MW00962133

ITALY TRAVEL GUIDE

Discover Italy: Your Ultimate Travel Guide to Italy's Best
Destinations, Hidden Gems, Cultural Treasures, and Culinary
Delightsfor a Truly Memorable Trip

Sasha Innammorati

© Copyright 2024 by Sasha Innammorati - All rights reserved.

The following Book is reproduced below with the goal of providing information that is as accurate and reliable as possible. Regardless, purchasing this Book can be seen as consent to the fact that both the publisher and the author of this book are in no way experts on the topics discussed within and that any recommendations or suggestions that are made herein are for entertainment purposes only. Professionals should be consulted as needed prior to undertaking any of the action endorsed herein.

This declaration is deemed fair and valid by both the American Bar Association and the Committee of Publishers Association and is legally binding throughout the United States.

Furthermore, the transmission, duplication, or reproduction of any of the following work including specific information will be considered an illegal act irrespective of if it is done electronically or in print. This extends to creating a secondary or tertiary copy of the work or a recorded copy and is only allowed with the express written consent from the Publisher. All additional right reserved.

The information in the following pages is broadly considered a truthful and accurate account of facts and as such, any inattention, use, or misuse of the information in question by the reader will render any resulting actions solely under their purview. There are no scenarios in which the publisher or the original author of this work can be in any fashion deemed liable for any hardship or damages that may befall them after undertaking information described herein.

Additionally, the information in the following pages is intended only for informational purposes and should thus be thought of as universal. As befitting its nature, it is presented without assurance regarding its prolonged validity or interim quality. Trademarks that are mentioned are done without written consent and can in no way be considered an endorsement from the trademark holde

Summary

Chapter 1: Introduction to Italy

1.1 Welcome to Italy

Welcome to Italy, a land where history, culture, and breathtaking landscapes come together to create an unparalleled travel experience. From the ancient ruins of Rome, where every stone whispers tales of bygone eras, to the romantic canals of Venice, which have inspired poets and lovers for centuries, Italy is a destination that captivates the heart and mind. As you embark on this journey, prepare to immerse yourself in a country renowned for its art, architecture, and culinary delights. Each region offers its own unique charm, ensuring that your visit to Italy will be as diverse as

it is memorable.

Whether you're wandering through the picturesque vineyards of Tuscany, savoring the fresh seafood along the Amalfi Coast, or exploring the medieval streets of Bologna, Italy promises an adventure that is as educational as it is enchanting. From the snow-capped peaks of the Dolomites to the sun-kissed beaches of Sicily, the country's varied landscapes provide a stunning backdrop for any type of traveler. Historical sites, world-class museums, and local festivals offer countless opportunities to dive deep into the essence of Italian culture. Prepare to be amazed by the vibrant street life, the warmth of its people, and the country's ability to seamlessly blend tradition with modernity.

1.2 Why Italy? An Overview of Its Rich History and Culture
Italy's rich history and culture make it a must-visit destination for travelers from around the world. With a legacy that spans from the grandeur of the Roman Empire to the artistic achievements of the Renaissance, Italy is a treasure trove of historical landmarks, artistic masterpieces, and vibrant traditions. In Rome, the Colosseum and the Pantheon stand as testaments to ancient engineering and architectural prowess. Florence, the birthplace of the Renaissance, houses unparalleled works of art by Michelangelo, Leonardo da Vinci, and Botticelli. Beyond the cities, Italy's diverse regions offer unique experiences—from the fashion-forward streets of Milan, the culinary delights of Bologna, to the serene countryside of Tuscany, where rolling hills and vineyards stretch as far as the eye can see. Each visit to Italy is a journey through time, where the past seamlessly intertwines with the present.

The influence of Italy's rich cultural heritage is evident in its architecture, language, and customs. The country's numerous UNESCO World Heritage sites, such as the archaeological ruins of Pompeii and the trulli houses of Alberobello, offer a glimpse into its storied past. Italian culture is also deeply rooted in its traditions and festivities, such as Carnevale in Venice, which showcases elaborate masks and costumes, and the Infiorata flower festivals, where streets are decorated with intricate floral designs. These cultural expressions highlight Italy's enduring commitment to celebrating beauty, craftsmanship, and communal spirit.

1.3 Travel Tips for First-Time Visitors

For first-time visitors, navigating Italy can be both exciting and overwhelming. To make the most of your trip, consider learning basic Italian phrases such as "grazie" (thank you) and "per favore" (please), which can go a long way in endearing you to locals. Italians appreciate when visitors make an effort to speak their language, even if it's just a few simple phrases. A friendly "buongiorno" (good morning) or "buonasera" (good evening) can also enhance your interactions and help you connect more meaningfully with the people you meet.

Carrying cash is advisable for small purchases, as some establishments may not accept credit cards. While major cities and tourist areas often have widespread card acceptance, smaller towns, local markets, and family-run businesses may prefer cash. ATMs (known locally as "bancomat") are widely available, but it's a good idea to have some euros on hand for convenience. Additionally, informing your bank of your travel plans can help avoid any issues with accessing your funds abroad.

Being mindful of local customs enhances your cultural experience. In Italy, greetings often include a handshake, and among friends and family, a kiss on both cheeks is common. Respecting these customs shows your appreciation for Italian culture. When entering shops, restaurants, or even elevators, a polite "buongiorno" or "buonasera" is customary and appreciated.

It's essential to be aware of peak tourist seasons, typically from June to August, and plan accordingly to avoid long queues and crowded attractions. During these months, popular destinations like Rome, Venice, and Florence can be very busy. Visiting popular sites early in the morning or late in the afternoon can help you enjoy these places with fewer crowds and cooler temperatures. Booking tickets in advance for major attractions such as the Colosseum, Uffizi Gallery, and Vatican Museums can save you time and ensure entry.

Understanding the regional differences in cuisine, dialects, and traditions can enrich your travel experience. Each region of Italy has its own distinct culinary specialties, from the rich pastas and meats of Emilia-Romagna to the fresh seafood and pesto of Liguria. Exploring local markets, known as "mercati," and trying regional dishes can provide a deeper appreciation of Italy's diverse food culture. Don't miss the opportunity to sample regional wines, cheeses, and other local products that vary greatly from one area to another.

Another tip is to make use of Italy's efficient public transportation system. Trains and buses connect major cities and smaller towns, making it easy to explore different regions without the need for a car. The train network, operated by Trenitalia and Italo, offers high-speed services between major cities and scenic regional routes. For instance, the train journey from Florence to Venice offers beautiful views of the Tuscan countryside and the Veneto region. Buses are useful for reaching more remote areas that are not serviced by trains.

However, renting a car can be advantageous for exploring rural areas and scenic drives, such as the Amalfi Coast or the Tuscan countryside. Driving in Italy allows you to discover charming villages, vineyards, and coastal roads at your own pace. Be aware of local driving regulations, such as the Zona a Traffico Limitato (ZTL) zones in city centers, which restrict access to non-resident vehicles. Parking can also be challenging in cities, so it's often best to park outside the center and use public transport or walk.

When dining out, understanding Italian meal times and etiquette can enhance your experience. Italians typically have a light breakfast, a substantial lunch between 1 PM and 3 PM, and a late dinner starting around 8 PM. Restaurants often close between lunch and dinner services, so plan your meals accordingly. Tipping is appreciated but not obligatory, as a service charge is often included in the bill. A small tip for exceptional service is always welcomed.

Staying connected is important for a smooth travel experience. Consider purchasing a local SIM card for your phone, which can provide better rates for data and local calls compared to international roaming plans. Major providers like TIM, Vodafone, and Wind have extensive coverage across the country. Free Wi-Fi is commonly available in hotels, cafes, and public places, but having mobile data can be useful for navigation and accessing travel information on the go.

Safety is another key aspect of travel. Italy is generally safe for tourists, but it's wise to take common-sense precautions. Be aware of your surroundings, especially in crowded areas, to avoid pickpocketing. Use a money belt or a cross-body bag with zippers for added security. Avoid carrying large amounts of cash and keep valuables secure. In case of emergency, the general emergency number in Italy is 112.

Finally, immerse yourself in the local culture by participating in local events and festivals. Italy's rich calendar of festivals, from food and wine fairs to historical reenactments and religious celebrations, offers unique insights into the local way of life. Engaging with locals, whether through a cooking class, a guided tour, or a casual conversation in a cafe, can provide a deeper understanding and appreciation of Italian culture.

By following these travel tips, you can navigate Italy with confidence and make the most of your visit. Whether you're marveling at ancient ruins, savoring regional delicacies, or simply enjoying the Italian way of life, your trip to Italy will be filled with unforgettable experiences and lasting memories.1.4 Planning Your Trip: When to Visit and What to Expect

Italy is a year-round destination, with each season offering its own distinct experiences. Spring (April to June) and autumn (September to October) are ideal for mild weather and fewer tourists, making it perfect for sightseeing and outdoor activities. Summer (July and August) is the peak tourist season, with warm weather ideal for beach vacations and vibrant festivals such as the Venice Film Festival and Siena's Palio. Winter (November to March) is quieter, offering the charm of Christmas markets, festive decorations, and skiing in the Alps. Regardless of when you visit, expect to be enchanted by Italy's timeless beauty, warm hospitality, and the rich tapestry of experiences that await you at every turn. Whether you're exploring the bustling cities or the tranquil countryside, Italy promises a trip filled with unforgettable moments and lasting memories.

In planning your trip, consider the regional climate and local events that may enhance your experience. For instance, visiting the Italian Riviera in the summer provides opportunities for beach activities and boat tours, while a winter visit to the Dolomites offers world-class skiing and cozy mountain lodges. Additionally, Italy's extensive rail network makes it easy to travel between cities and regions, allowing you to maximize your time and explore more of this captivating country. Booking accommodations in advance, especially during peak seasons, can ensure you have a comfortable base from which to explore. With thoughtful planning and a spirit of adventure, your Italian journey will undoubtedly be a memorable and enriching experience.

Chapter 2: Iconic Destinations

2.1 Rome: The Eternal City

Rome, often referred to as "The Eternal City," is a destination that epitomizes the grandeur of ancient civilizations and the vibrancy of modern urban life. As Italy's capital, Rome seamlessly blends its historic legacy with contemporary culture, offering a dynamic and captivating experience for every visitor. Walking through the streets of Rome is like stepping into a living museum, where every corner reveals layers of history, from ancient ruins to Renaissance art and Baroque architecture. The city's rich past and vibrant present coexist, creating an atmosphere that is both timeless and exciting.

Ancient Rome: A Journey Through Time

Rome's ancient roots are undeniably its most compelling feature. The city's origins date back to 753 BC, and it was the heart of the Roman Empire, which ruled vast territories across Europe, Asia, and Africa. The Colosseum is perhaps the most iconic symbol of ancient Rome. This massive amphitheater once hosted gladiatorial contests, public spectacles, and dramas. Walking through its arches, visitors can almost hear the echoes of the roaring crowds and the clash of swords. The Colosseum stands as a testament to Roman engineering prowess and the grandeur of its entertainment culture.

Nearby, the Roman Forum offers a glimpse into the political and social heart of ancient Rome. This sprawling complex of ruins includes temples, basilicas, and public spaces that were once bustling with activity. Key sites within the Forum include the Temple of Saturn, the Arch of Titus, and the House of the Vestal Virgins. Each structure tells a story of Rome's glory days, from its early Republic to its imperial zenith. Walking along the Via Sacra, the main thoroughfare of the Forum, visitors can imagine the processions and public life that once filled these ancient streets.

The Pantheon, another architectural marvel from ancient Rome, is one of the best-preserved buildings from that era. Originally built as a temple to all the gods, it has been used as a Christian church since the 7th century. Its massive dome, with a central oculus that lets in natural light, remains an engineering wonder. The Pantheon's harmonious proportions and grandeur have inspired architects for centuries.

Renaissance and Baroque Splendors

While ancient Rome's remnants dominate the landscape, the city is also renowned for its Renaissance and Baroque art and architecture. The Vatican City, an independent city-state within Rome, is the spiritual and administrative center of the Roman Catholic Church. Here, visitors can marvel at the opulence of St. Peter's Basilica, designed by some of the greatest architects of the Renaissance, including Michelangelo, who also designed its iconic dome. The basilica's interior is adorned with masterpieces such as Michelangelo's Pietà and Bernini's Baldachin.

The Sistine Chapel, located within the Vatican Museums, is another highlight. Michelangelo's frescoes on the chapel's ceiling and the Last Judgment on the altar wall are considered some of the greatest achievements in Western art. The Vatican Museums themselves house an extensive collection of art, from classical sculptures to Renaissance paintings, offering a comprehensive journey through art history.

Rome's Baroque period is epitomized by the Trevi Fountain, a masterpiece of sculpture and architecture. Designed by Nicola Salvi and completed by Giuseppe Pannini, this monumental fountain is a favorite among visitors. The tradition of tossing a coin into the fountain to ensure a return to Rome adds a touch of magic to the experience. Nearby, the Spanish Steps provide another iconic Roman scene. This grand staircase, leading up to the Trinità dei Monti church, is a popular spot for both relaxation and people-watching.

The Piazza Navona is a splendid example of Baroque architecture and urban design. Built on the site of the ancient Stadium of Domitian, this lively square features Bernini's Fountain of the Four Rivers, representing the major rivers of the four continents known at the time. The piazza is surrounded by historic buildings and is home to numerous cafes and street performers, making it a vibrant and atmospheric place to visit.

Modern Rome: A Vibrant Metropolis

Modern Rome is a bustling metropolis that retains its historical charm while embracing contemporary life. The city is a major center for fashion, politics, and culture. Via Condotti and the surrounding streets near the Spanish Steps are home to some of the world's most luxurious fashion boutiques. High-end Italian brands such as Gucci, Prada, and Valentino have their flagship stores here, attracting fashion enthusiasts from around the globe.

Rome's culinary scene is equally impressive, blending traditional Italian cuisine with modern gastronomic trends. Trattorias and osterias serve classic dishes like carbonara, amatriciana, and cacio e pepe, while contemporary restaurants experiment with new flavors and techniques. The city's markets, such as the Campo de' Fiori and Mercato di Testaccio, offer a taste of local produce, cheeses, and cured meats, reflecting the richness of Roman culinary traditions.

The city's vibrant nightlife includes a range of options from wine bars and cafes to nightclubs and live music venues. Areas like Trastevere and Monti are particularly popular for their lively atmospheres and eclectic mix of bars and eateries. These neighborhoods offer a blend of historic charm and modern vibrancy, making them perfect for evening strolls and socializing.

Cultural Festivals and Events

Rome hosts numerous cultural festivals and events throughout the year that highlight its diverse heritage and contemporary dynamism. The Rome Film Fest attracts international filmmakers and celebrities, showcasing the best in global cinema. Estate Romana, a summer festival, features outdoor concerts, theater performances, and film screenings in some of the city's most beautiful locations, including the banks of the Tiber River and the ruins of ancient sites.

Religious events also play a significant role in Rome's cultural calendar. Easter and Christmas are celebrated with grand ceremonies at St. Peter's Basilica, attracting pilgrims and visitors from around the world. The Feast of Saints Peter and Paul, the city's patron saints, is marked by processions, fireworks, and special masses.

Hidden Gems and Local Life

Beyond the well-trodden tourist paths, Rome is filled with hidden gems waiting to be discovered. Neighborhoods like Testaccio, once the city's meatpacking district, are now vibrant areas known for their food markets and nightlife. The Aventine Hill offers a quieter, more residential side of Rome, with its beautiful gardens and the famous keyhole view of St. Peter's Basilica.

The Appian Way, one of the oldest roads in Rome, provides a scenic and historic route for walking or cycling. Along the way, visitors can explore ancient catacombs, aqueducts, and the remains of Roman villas. The Janiculum Hill offers stunning panoramic views of the city, making it a perfect spot for a relaxing afternoon.

Rome's local life is characterized by a strong sense of community and tradition. Small family-owned businesses, cafes, and artisan workshops are integral parts of the city's fabric. Exploring these local establishments offers a glimpse into the daily life of Romans and the enduring traditions that define their culture.

Conclusion

Rome, with its unparalleled blend of ancient history and vibrant modernity, offers a captivating experience for every visitor. Its grand monuments, world-renowned art, bustling markets, and charming neighborhoods create a rich tapestry of sights, sounds, and flavors. Whether exploring the ruins of the Roman Empire, admiring Renaissance masterpieces, or enjoying contemporary Italian cuisine, visitors to Rome are sure to be enchanted by the Eternal City's timeless allure and dynamic spirit.2.1.1 Must-See Landmarks: Colosseum, Vatican City, and More

No visit to Rome is complete without exploring its iconic landmarks. The Colosseum, an architectural marvel and symbol of ancient Roman engineering, invites you to step back in time and imagine the gladiatorial combats that once entertained thousands. Nearby, the Roman Forum presents a sprawling complex of ruins that were once the heart of political and social life in ancient Rome. The sense of history and the scale of these structures provide a profound insight into the grandeur of the Roman Empire.

Vatican City, an independent city-state within Rome, is the spiritual and administrative center of the Roman Catholic Church. Here, you can marvel at the opulence of St. Peter's

Basilica, the artistic genius of Michelangelo's Sistine Chapel ceiling, and the vast collections of the Vatican Museums. The grandeur and historical significance of these sites make them essential stops on any Roman itinerary. Visitors often find themselves in awe of the sheer beauty and craftsmanship on display, making Vatican City a highlight of any trip to Rome.

In addition to these world-renowned attractions, Rome offers numerous other landmarks. The Pantheon, with its remarkable dome and oculus, exemplifies ancient architectural prowess. The Trevi Fountain, a Baroque masterpiece, not only dazzles with its beauty but also offers a chance to partake in the tradition of tossing a coin to ensure a return to Rome. The Spanish Steps provide a picturesque spot for relaxation and people-watching, while the bustling Piazza Navona showcases stunning fountains and lively street performances. Each of these sites contributes to the rich tapestry of experiences that Rome offers, ensuring that visitors can immerse themselves in the city's vibrant history and culture.

2.1.2 Family-Friendly Activities in Rome
Rome is not only a haven for history buffs but also a fantastic destination for families. The city offers a variety of activities that cater to all ages, ensuring an enjoyable experience for both parents and children. Rome's family-friendly attractions are designed to engage and educate, making it an ideal destination for a fun and enriching vacation.

For a fun and educational experience, visit Explora, the Children's Museum of Rome. This interactive museum allows kids to engage with exhibits that cover topics from science and technology to art and nature. It's a great way for young minds to learn through play and discovery. The museum's hands-on approach ensures that children remain captivated and curious throughout their visit. Exhibits are designed to be interactive and educational, providing an immersive experience that combines fun with learning. Workshops and special events held at the museum further enhance the educational experience, making it a must-visit for families.

Another family-friendly attraction is the Bioparco di Roma, the city's zoological park. Home to over a thousand animals from around the world, the zoo provides an opportunity to learn about wildlife conservation while enjoying a day surrounded by nature. The lush Villa Borghese Gardens, where the zoo is located, also offers playgrounds, bike rentals, and picnic areas, making it a perfect spot for a family outing. The expansive gardens provide a peaceful retreat from the hustle and bustle of the city, where families can relax and enjoy outdoor activities together. The park's attractions include a boating lake, puppet theater, and horse-drawn carriage rides, offering various ways to explore and enjoy the green space.

Rome's many gelaterias are a hit with children and adults alike. Sampling authentic Italian gelato is a must, and many gelaterias offer a wide variety of flavors to satisfy every palate. For a hands-on experience, some gelato shops even offer workshops where families can learn the art of making this delicious treat. These workshops provide a fun and tasty way for families to engage with Italian culture and cuisine. Exploring different flavors and understanding the process behind making gelato can be a delightful educational experience for kids.

Exploring Rome by foot can be tiring for little ones, but a hop-on-hop-off bus tour provides a convenient and exciting way to see the city's top attractions without exhausting young travelers. These tours offer informative commentary and the flexibility to explore at your own pace. The buses stop at major landmarks, allowing families to hop off and explore before continuing their journey. This mode of transportation is particularly useful for covering more ground without the strain of walking long distances, and it allows for a comfortable way to take in the sights and sounds of Rome.

For a more adventurous option, families can consider renting bicycles or pedal cars available in Villa Borghese and other parks. This can be a fun way to explore larger areas while enjoying a bit of exercise. Many parks also have designated paths for cycling, ensuring safety for young riders.

Rome's historical sites also cater to younger visitors through specially designed tours and activities. The Colosseum, for example, offers family-friendly tours that focus on the gladiatorial games and daily life in ancient Rome, often including interactive elements and storytelling to keep children engaged. Similarly, the Vatican Museums offer family-friendly itineraries that highlight key artworks and include treasure hunts to make the experience more engaging for kids.

Lastly, don't miss the opportunity to take a leisurely stroll along the Tiber River. The riverbanks are lined with cafes and markets, and the calm waters provide a peaceful contrast to the bustling city streets. It's an ideal place for a relaxing2.2 Venice: The City of Canals

Venice, the enchanting City of Canals, captivates visitors with its unique charm and timeless beauty. Built on a network of canals, this floating city is a masterpiece of architecture and engineering, offering an unparalleled romantic experience. Venice's labyrinth of waterways, bridges, and narrow streets creates a magical atmosphere that has inspired artists, writers, and travelers for centuries.

2.2.1 Top Attractions: St. Mark's Basilica, Grand Canal

St. Mark's Basilica, with its stunning mosaics and opulent design, is a must-see. Located in the heart of St. Mark's Square, it epitomizes Venetian grandeur. The basilica's intricate facade and richly decorated interior reflect the city's historical wealth and artistic achievement. Visitors can also climb the campanile, or bell tower, for panoramic views of the city and the lagoon.

The Grand Canal, Venice's main waterway, is lined with historic buildings and bustling with gondolas and vaporettos. A ride along the Grand Canal offers breathtaking views of iconic structures like the Rialto Bridge and Ca' d'Oro. The canal serves as the city's main thoroughfare, providing a unique perspective on Venetian life and architecture. Cruising along the Grand Canal allows visitors to appreciate the grandeur of Venice's palaces and the vibrant activity of its waterfront.

2.2.2 Gondola Rides and Hidden Corners

Gondola rides are quintessential to the Venetian experience. Gliding through the narrow canals, visitors can explore the city's hidden corners and lesser-known gems, such as charming bridges and secluded squares. Each gondola ride offers a unique perspective, revealing Venice's hidden beauty and tranquil ambiance. Gondoliers often share stories and insights about the city, enhancing the romantic and mystical experience of exploring Venice by water.

Beyond the main tourist paths, Venice is filled with hidden treasures waiting to be discovered. Wandering through the backstreets and lesser-known neighborhoods, visitors can stumble upon quiet squares, artisanal shops, and local cafes. Areas like Cannaregio and Dorsoduro offer a more authentic glimpse into everyday Venetian life, away from the bustling crowds of St. Mark's Square.

2.3 Florence: The Birthplace of the Renaissance

Florence, the cradle of the Renaissance, is a treasure trove of art and architecture. This historic city is renowned for its contributions to art, culture, and humanism, making it a must-visit for any art enthusiast. Florence's streets are like an open-air museum, filled with masterpieces from some of history's greatest artists and architects.

2.3.1 Art and Architecture Highlights

Florence is home to some of the world's most significant art and architectural landmarks. The city's contributions to the Renaissance and its influence on Western art and culture are unparalleled, making it a must-visit destination for art enthusiasts and history buffs alike.

The Florence Cathedral and Brunelleschi's Dome

The Florence Cathedral, also known as the Duomo di Firenze or Santa Maria del Fiore, is an architectural masterpiece that dominates the city's skyline. Designed by Arnolfo di Cambio and completed by Filippo Brunelleschi, its iconic dome is a feat of engineering and a symbol of the Renaissance. The cathedral's intricate facade, adorned with green, pink, and white marble, sets the stage for the grandeur within. Inside, visitors are greeted by the vast interior, which includes stunning frescoes by Giorgio Vasari and Federico Zuccari that adorn the dome's interior.

Brunelleschi's dome itself is a marvel, not just for its size but for the ingenuity involved in its construction. The dome was built without the use of scaffolding, using a herringbone brick pattern and a double shell structure, techniques that were revolutionary at the time. Visitors can climb to the top of the dome for a panoramic view of Florence, a journey that also provides an up-close look at the frescoes and the dome's architectural details.

Palazzo Vecchio

The Palazzo Vecchio is another symbol of Florence's historical and political significance. Serving as the town hall, this fortress-like palace overlooks the Piazza della Signoria, a square filled with sculptures including a replica of Michelangelo's David. The palazzo itself houses the Salone dei Cinquecento, a grand hall decorated with frescoes depicting the city's military victories and political power. Visitors can explore various rooms adorned with works by Vasari, Donatello, and other prominent artists of the time.

The tower of Palazzo Vecchio, known as Torre di Arnolfo, offers another vantage point for spectacular views of the city. The building's rich history is palpable, as it was the heart of Florence's political life during the Renaissance and continues to be a center of civic activity.

Michelangelo's David and the Galleria dell'Accademia

The Galleria dell'Accademia is home to one of the most famous sculptures in the world, Michelangelo's David. This iconic statue represents the biblical hero David and is celebrated for its detailed portrayal of the human form and its embodiment of Renaissance ideals of beauty and proportion. Standing at over 14 feet tall, David is carved from a single block of marble and depicts the moment before his battle with Goliath, capturing a sense of tension and focus.

In addition to David, the Galleria dell'Accademia houses other important works by Michelangelo, including his unfinished Prisoners (or Slaves), which provide insight into his artistic process. The museum also features a collection of Renaissance paintings, musical instruments, and Gothic altarpieces, making it a comprehensive repository of art from the period.

The Uffizi Gallery

The Uffizi Gallery is one of the most renowned art museums in the world, housing an unparalleled collection of Renaissance masterpieces. Founded by the Medici family, the gallery's extensive collection includes works by Sandro Botticelli, Leonardo da Vinci, Raphael, Titian, and Caravaggio. Botticelli's The Birth of Venus and Primavera are among the highlights, celebrated for their mythological themes and delicate beauty.

The gallery itself, designed by Giorgio Vasari, is an architectural marvel, featuring long corridors lined with sculptures and rooms filled with some of the most significant works of art from the 14th to the 18th century. The Uffizi offers an immersive journey through the development of Renaissance art, showcasing the evolution of artistic techniques and styles.

Ponte Vecchio

The Ponte Vecchio, a medieval stone bridge spanning the Arno River, is one of Florence's most iconic landmarks. Famous for its shops built along the bridge, a tradition dating back to the 13th century, the Ponte Vecchio is lined with jewelry shops, art dealers, and souvenir sellers. The bridge's distinctive design, with its three arches, has made it a symbol of Florence. Historically, it was the only bridge across the Arno that survived

World War II, thanks to an order by Hitler to spare it during the German retreat.

Basilica of Santa Croce

The Basilica of Santa Croce is another architectural gem and a significant historical site. Known as the Temple of the Italian Glories, it is the burial place of some of Italy's most illustrious figures, including Michelangelo, Galileo, Machiavelli, and Rossini. The basilica's Gothic exterior, with its striking white and green marble facade, leads into an interior filled with beautiful frescoes by Giotto and his pupils, depicting scenes from the lives of St. Francis and other saints.

The basilica also houses a museum that includes works by Donatello and exhibits related to the history of the church and its notable burials. The Pazzi Chapel, designed by Brunelleschi, is an example of early Renaissance architecture and can be found in the basilica's cloister.

Other Notable Sites

Florence's artistic and architectural treasures extend beyond these well-known landmarks. The Bargello Museum, housed in a medieval fortress, contains an important collection of Renaissance sculptures, including works by Donatello and Verrocchio. The Medici Chapels, part of the Basilica of San Lorenzo, are another highlight, featuring Michelangelo's sculptures in the New Sacristy.

The Boboli Gardens, behind the Pitti Palace, offer a green oasis filled with statues, fountains, and grottoes, reflecting the

Renaissance ideal of harmonizing nature and art. The Palazzo Pitti itself houses several museums, including the Palatine Gallery, which features works by Raphael, Titian, and Rubens, and the Museum of Modern Art, showcasing Italian art from the 18th to the 20th centuries.

Florence's rich tapestry of art and architecture ensures that every visitor can find inspiration and awe in its streets and museums. The city's commitment to preserving its cultural heritage makes it a living museum, where the Renaissance spirit continues to thrive. Whether exploring the grandeur of the Duomo, the artistic treasures of the Uffizi, or the serene beauty of the Boboli Gardens, Florence offers an unparalleled journey through the history of art and architecture.

2.3.2 Best Museums and Galleries for Families
Florence offers numerous museums and galleries that cater to families, ensuring an educational and enjoyable experience for visitors of all ages. The city's rich cultural heritage is presented in a way that captivates both adults and children, making it an ideal destination for family vacations.

Leonardo da Vinci Museum

The Leonardo da Vinci Museum is a fantastic destination for families, featuring interactive exhibits that engage children with Leonardo's inventions and artworks. Located in the heart of Florence, the museum offers a hands-on approach to learning about one of the greatest geniuses in history. The exhibits include life-sized models of Leonardo's inventions, which children can manipulate to understand the principles of mechanics, flight, and hydraulics. This interactive experience allows young visitors to explore Leonardo's genius in a fun and educational way, fostering curiosity and a love for science and art.

Museo Galileo

The Museo Galileo, dedicated to the history of science, is another excellent choice for families. The museum's collection includes scientific instruments from the Renaissance period, many of which were used by Galileo Galilei himself. Hands-on exhibits captivate young minds, allowing children to interact with replicas of historical instruments and understand their functions. The museum also offers educational workshops and activities designed specifically for children, making complex scientific concepts accessible and engaging. These experiences provide a fascinating insight into the scientific advancements of the Renaissance and the impact of Galileo's discoveries on the world.

The Boboli Gardens

In addition to indoor attractions, Florence's Boboli Gardens provide a beautiful outdoor space for families to explore. These historic gardens are filled with sculptures, fountains, and manicured landscapes, offering a peaceful retreat in the heart of the city. Families can enjoy picnics, leisurely walks, and the stunning views of Florence from the gardens' elevated points. The expansive grounds of the Boboli Gardens feature winding pathways, hidden grottos, and an amphitheater, providing endless opportunities for children to explore and discover. The gardens are not only a place of beauty but also a living museum of Renaissance landscape design.

Palazzo Vecchio

The Palazzo Vecchio, Florence's historic town hall, also offers family-friendly activities. The museum within the palazzo includes interactive tours and workshops designed for children, such as costume tours where kids can dress up in Renaissance attire and learn about the life of a Medici prince or princess. The Secret Passages Tour takes families through hidden staircases and secret rooms, providing an adventurous and educational exploration of the palazzo's history and architecture.

The Uffizi Gallery

While the Uffizi Gallery might seem like a more adult-oriented destination, it has made significant efforts to become family-friendly. The gallery offers guided tours tailored for children, focusing on engaging stories behind the masterpieces and interactive activities that keep young visitors entertained. Special family guides and activity booklets are available, helping children to understand and appreciate the art in a fun and meaningful way.

Museo degli Innocenti

Another notable museum for families is the Museo degli Innocenti, which tells the story of the Ospedale degli Innocenti, a historic orphanage in Florence. The museum's exhibits are designed to be engaging for children, with multimedia displays and interactive elements that explain the history of the institution and the lives of the children who lived there. The museum also includes a dedicated children's area with educational games and activities.

Stibbert Museum

The Stibbert Museum is a lesser-known gem that appeals to families with its eclectic collection of arms, armor, and costumes from around the world. The museum's exhibits are displayed in a way that feels like a journey through time, with rooms dedicated to different historical periods and cultures. Children are often fascinated by the suits of armor, weaponry, and elaborate costumes, making it a captivating experience for the whole family.

Palazzo Strozzi

Palazzo Strozzi often hosts exhibitions that include interactive elements and workshops for children. The museum's Family Kit, available for certain exhibitions, provides tools and activities to help young visitors engage with the art on display. These resources are designed to make the museum experience enjoyable and educational for families.

The Children's Museum at Palazzo Vecchio

Within the Palazzo Vecchio, the Children's Museum offers a space specifically designed for young visitors. Interactive exhibits and workshops focus on the history of Florence and the Medici family, using storytelling and hands-on activities to bring the past to life. The museum's programs are designed to be both fun and educational, ensuring that children leave with a deeper understanding of Florence's rich history.

Florence's blend of artistic heritage and family-friendly attractions ensures that every visitor, regardless of age, can find something to inspire and delight them. The city's rich cultural offerings, combined with its welcoming atmosphere, make it a perfect destination for a family vacation. From interactive science exhibits and Renaissance art to beautiful gardens and historic palaces, Florence provides a diverse range of experiences that cater to families, ensuring that both children and adults have a memorable and enriching visit.

Chapter 3: Hidden Gems

3.1 Exploring Lesser-Known Villages

Italy is a country abundant with hidden gems, many of which are nestled in its lesser-known villages. These quaint locations provide a unique glimpse into the authentic, everyday life of Italians, away from the crowded tourist spots and bustling cities. Exploring these villages allows travelers to experience Italy's rich culture and traditions in a more intimate and relaxed setting. Two such destinations that epitomize the charm and historical depth of Italy are Cinque Terre and Matera.

Cinque Terre: A Coastal Treasure

Cinque Terre, a breathtaking coastal area in the Liguria region, comprises five picturesque villages: Monterosso al Mare, Vernazza, Corniglia, Manarola, and Riomaggiore. This UNESCO World Heritage site is renowned for its colorful houses perched on rugged cliffs overlooking the Mediterranean Sea. Each village offers stunning views, charming streets, and a relaxed pace of life that epitomizes the essence of coastal Italy.

Monterosso al Mare, the largest of the five villages, is known for its beautiful beaches and historical landmarks, including the Church of San Giovanni Battista. Its expansive sandy beach makes it a popular spot for sunbathing and swimming, while its old town is filled with quaint shops and restaurants offering delicious Ligurian cuisine. The village is also famous for its lemon trees and locally produced lemon products, such as Limoncino.

Vernazza, often considered the most picturesque, boasts a natural harbor, vibrant streets, and the medieval Belforte Tower. The harbor is a perfect spot for a leisurely lunch with a view, while the narrow streets are lined with colorful houses and small eateries serving fresh seafood. Vernazza's charm lies in its lively atmosphere and stunning coastal scenery, making it a favorite among photographers.

Corniglia, perched high above the sea, offers panoramic views and a quieter atmosphere. Unlike the other villages, Corniglia is not directly adjacent to the sea, giving it a more tranquil feel. The village is accessible by a steep staircase known as the Lardarina or by a shuttle bus from the train station. Corniglia's peaceful streets, terraced vineyards, and quaint cafes provide a serene escape from the busier coastal towns.

Manarola, with its charming waterfront and terraced vineyards, is a favorite for photographers. The village's iconic cliffside views are often featured in postcards and travel guides. Manarola is also known for its sweet Sciacchetrà wine, made from sun-dried grapes grown on the steep terraces surrounding the village. The picturesque harbor is perfect for swimming and exploring the local marine life.

Riomaggiore's steep streets and colorful buildings provide a quintessential Cinque Terre experience. The village's narrow alleys are filled with character, offering hidden gems like artisanal shops and local trattorias. Riomaggiore's marina is bustling with fishing boats, and the surrounding hills offer hiking trails with spectacular views of the coastline.

Hiking trails connect these villages, offering adventurous ways to explore the region's natural beauty. The Sentiero Azzurro (Blue Trail) is the most famous, winding along the coastline and providing breathtaking vistas at every turn. This trail allows hikers to traverse the stunning landscapes between the villages, enjoying the dramatic cliffs and vibrant flora along the way. For those seeking a more challenging hike, the Sentiero Rosso (Red Trail) runs higher up in the hills, offering even more spectacular views and a quieter path.

Beyond the trails, visitors can indulge in fresh seafood, sample local wines such as Sciacchetrà, and immerse themselves in the laid-back lifestyle that defines this coastal treasure. Each village has its own unique character and charm, making Cinque Terre a diverse and enchanting destination. Boat tours and kayaking excursions provide alternative ways to explore the stunning coastline, offering different perspectives of the picturesque villages.

Matera: The Ancient Cave City

Matera, located in the region of Basilicata, is renowned for its ancient cave dwellings known as "Sassi." These cave structures, some of which date back over 9,000 years, have been transformed into homes, hotels, and restaurants, making Matera a fascinating destination that seamlessly blends history and modernity. The Sassi of Matera are divided into two districts: Sasso Caveoso and Sasso Barisano, each offering a unique exploration of ancient living quarters carved into the limestone.

Walking through Matera's narrow streets and alleys feels like stepping back in time. The city's unique landscape, with its labyrinthine layout and stone-carved buildings, showcases the ingenuity and resilience of past civilizations. Visitors can explore cave churches adorned with ancient frescoes, such as the Crypt of Original Sin, known as the "Sistine Chapel of Rupestrian Art," and the Church of San Pietro Barisano, which features an intricate underground labyrinth. These churches provide a fascinating insight into the spiritual life of the ancient inhabitants and are testament to the region's rich religious history.

Matera's historical significance extends beyond its architecture. The city has been continuously inhabited for millennia, making it one of the oldest living cities in the world. Its recent designation as a European Capital of Culture in 2019 has brought renewed interest and investment, further enhancing its appeal as a travel destination. Whether staying in a cave hotel or dining in a cave restaurant, Matera offers a truly immersive and unforgettable experience. The blend of ancient traditions and contemporary comforts creates a unique atmosphere that captivates every visitor.

In addition to its historical attractions, Matera offers various cultural events and festivals throughout the year. The Matera Film Festival and the Festa della Bruna are notable events that celebrate the city's cultural heritage and attract visitors from around the world. These events provide a lively and festive backdrop to the serene and timeless beauty of Matera.

Exploring Matera also means delving into its culinary delights. The region's cuisine is rich in flavors and traditions, with dishes such as orecchiette pasta, lamb stew, and fresh ricotta. Local markets and traditional restaurants offer a taste of authentic Basilicata, where visitors can enjoy hearty meals made from locally sourced ingredients.

Conclusion

Exploring lesser-known villages like Cinque Terre and Matera offers a deeper, more intimate connection to Italy's rich cultural and historical heritage. These destinations provide a refreshing alternative to the typical tourist routes, allowing travelers to experience the authentic charm and tranquility of Italian life. Whether wandering the colorful streets of Cinque Terre or exploring the ancient cave dwellings of Matera, visitors are sure to be enchanted by the unique beauty and timeless appeal of these hidden gems. Italy's lesser-known villages offer a glimpse into the heart and soul of the country, making them a must-visit for those seeking a truly memorable and enriching travel experience.

3.1.1 Cinque Terre: A Coastal Treasure

Cinque Terre, a breathtaking coastal area in the Liguria region, comprises five picturesque villages: Monterosso al Mare, Vernazza, Corniglia, Manarola, and Riomaggiore. This UNESCO World Heritage site is renowned for its colorful houses perched on rugged cliffs overlooking the Mediterranean Sea. Each village offers stunning views, charming streets, and a relaxed pace of life that epitomizes the essence of coastal Italy.

Monterosso al Mare, the largest of the five villages, is known for its beautiful beaches and historical landmarks, including the Church of San Giovanni Battista. Its expansive sandy beach makes it a popular spot for sunbathing and swimming, while its old town is filled with quaint shops and restaurants. Vernazza, often considered the most picturesque, boasts a natural harbor, vibrant streets, and the medieval Belforte Tower. The village is famous for its brightly colored houses and its lively piazza by the waterfront, where visitors can enjoy fresh seafood and local wines.

Corniglia, perched high above the sea, offers panoramic views and a quieter atmosphere. Unlike the other villages, Corniglia is not directly adjacent to the sea, which makes it less crowded and more serene. Its narrow streets and terraced vineyards provide a peaceful retreat for those looking to escape the hustle and bustle. Manarola, with its charming waterfront and terraced vineyards, is a favorite for photographers. The village's iconic cliffside views are often featured in postcards and travel guides, and its local wine, Sciacchetrà, is a must-try. Riomaggiore's steep streets and colorful buildings provide a quintessential Cinque Terre experience, with its marina offering picturesque views of fishing boats bobbing in the harbor.

Hiking trails connect these villages, offering adventurous ways to explore the region's natural beauty. The Sentiero Azzurro (Blue Trail) is the most famous, winding along the coastline and providing breathtaking vistas at every turn. Beyond the trails, visitors can indulge in fresh seafood, sample local wines such as Sciacchetrà, and immerse themselves in the laid-back lifestyle that defines this coastal treasure. Each village has its own unique character and charm, making Cinque Terre a diverse and enchanting destination.

3.1.2 Matera: The Ancient Cave City
Matera, located in the region of Basilicata, is renowned for its ancient cave dwellings known as "Sassi." These cave structures, some of which date back over 9,000 years, have been transformed into homes, hotels, and restaurants, making Matera a fascinating destination that seamlessly blends history and modernity. The Sassi of Matera are divided into two districts: Sasso Caveoso and Sasso Barisano, each offering a unique exploration of ancient living quarters carved into the limestone.

Walking through Matera's narrow streets and alleys feels like stepping back in time. The city's unique landscape, with its labyrinthine layout and stone-carved buildings, showcases the ingenuity and resilience of past civilizations. Visitors can explore cave churches adorned with ancient frescoes, such as the Crypt of Original Sin, known as the "Sistine Chapel of Rupestrian Art," and the Church of San Pietro Barisano, which features an intricate underground labyrinth. These churches provide a fascinating insight into the spiritual life of the ancient inhabitants and are testament to the region's rich religious history.

Matera's historical significance extends beyond its architecture. The city has been continuously inhabited for millennia, making it one of the oldest living cities in the world. Its recent designation as a European Capital of Culture in 2019 has brought renewed interest and investment, further enhancing its appeal as a travel destination. Whether staying in a cave hotel or dining in a cave restaurant, Matera offers a truly immersive and unforgettable experience. The blend of ancient traditions and contemporary comforts creates a unique atmosphere that captivates every visitor.

In addition to its historical attractions, Matera offers various cultural events and festivals throughout the year. The Matera Film Festival and the Festa della Bruna are notable events that celebrate the city's cultural heritage and attract visitors from all over the world. These events provide a lively and festive backdrop to the serene and timeless beauty of Matera.

3.2 Off-the-Beaten-Path Experiences
For those seeking unique and immersive experiences, Italy offers numerous off-the-beaten-path adventures that go beyond the usual tourist itineraries. Two particularly enriching activities are truffle hunting in Piedmont and wine tasting tours in Tuscany.

3.2.1 Truffle Hunting in Piedmont
Piedmont, a region in northern Italy, is famous for its truffles, particularly the highly prized white truffle from Alba. Truffle hunting, often accompanied by trained dogs, is an exciting and rewarding activity that allows visitors to explore the picturesque countryside while searching for these elusive fungi. The experience typically starts early in the morning, as hunters and

their dogs roam the forests and hillsides, guided by the dogs' keen sense of smell.

Participating in a truffle hunt provides insight into this traditional practice and the skill required to unearth these culinary treasures. After the hunt, visitors are often treated to a tasting of freshly found truffles paired with local delicacies, such as pasta, risotto, or eggs, accompanied by regional wines. This immersive experience not only highlights the region's gastronomic excellence but also fosters an appreciation for the delicate balance between nature and tradition.

In addition to truffle hunting, Piedmont offers a wealth of gastronomic experiences. The region is known for its rich cuisine, featuring dishes like bagna càuda, vitello tonnato, and agnolotti del plin. Exploring local markets and dining in traditional trattorias provides a deeper understanding of Piedmont's culinary heritage. The region's wines, such as Barolo and Barbaresco, are also world-renowned, and visiting local wineries for tastings and tours is a must for any food and wine enthusiast.

3.2.2 Wine Tasting Tours in Tuscany
Tuscany's rolling hills and vineyards are synonymous with world-class wines, making it an ideal destination for wine enthusiasts. Wine tasting tours in this region offer an intimate and educational experience of Italy's viniculture. Visitors can tour historic wineries, learn about the winemaking process, and sample a variety of wines, including the renowned Chianti, Brunello di Montalcino, and Vino Nobile di Montepulciano.

These tours often include food pairings, enhancing the tasting experience and providing a deeper appreciation of Tuscany's culinary heritage. Many wineries also offer cooking classes, vineyard walks, and cellar tours, allowing visitors to fully immerse themselves in the winemaking tradition. The combination of Tuscany's scenic beauty, rich history, and exceptional wines makes for a memorable and enriching experience.

In addition to wine tasting, Tuscany offers a variety of other activities that allow visitors to connect with the region's culture and landscape. Hot air balloon rides over the vineyards, cycling tours through the countryside, and cooking classes focused on traditional Tuscan cuisine are just a few of the experiences that await. The region's historic towns, such as Siena, San Gimignano, and Pienza, provide additional opportunities for exploration and discovery.

Conclusion

Italy's hidden gems, from the coastal splendor of Cinque Terre to the ancient cave city of Matera, along with unique off-the-beaten-path experiences like truffle hunting in Piedmont and wine tasting in Tuscany, offer travelers a deeper, more authentic connection to the country's rich cultural and natural heritage. These destinations and activities provide a refreshing alternative to the typical tourist routes, ensuring a truly unforgettable journey.

Whether you're exploring the colorful villages of Cinque Terre, delving into the ancient history of Matera, hunting for truffles in the forests of Piedmont, or savoring fine wines in the vineyards of Tuscany, these experiences allow you to see Italy in a new and more personal light. They offer a chance to slow down, connect with locals, and appreciate the beauty and diversity of this incredible country. Italy's hidden gems are waiting to be discovered, promising adventures that are as enriching as they are memorable.

Chapter 4: Cultural Treasures

4.1 Italian Art and Architecture

Italy's rich cultural heritage is epitomized by its art and architecture, spanning centuries and influencing global artistic movements. The country's contributions to the arts are monumental, shaping the aesthetics and techniques of various periods, from ancient Roman times to the Renaissance and beyond.

4.1.1 Masterpieces of the Renaissance

The Renaissance, born in Italy during the 14th to the 17th centuries, produced some of the world's most renowned masterpieces, fundamentally transforming Western art and thought. Florence, often considered the heart of this cultural rebirth, boasts iconic works such as Michelangelo's David, a stunning representation of human perfection, and Botticelli's The Birth of Venus in the Uffizi Gallery, which captures the ethereal beauty of mythological themes.

In Rome, the Sistine Chapel ceiling by Michelangelo is a monumental achievement in art, depicting scenes from the Book of Genesis with incredible detail and dynamism. Equally impressive are Raphael's frescoes in the Vatican Museums, particularly The School of Athens, which celebrates the classical spirit of inquiry and humanism. These masterpieces showcase the innovation, skill, and beauty that define Renaissance art, offering visitors a profound appreciation of this transformative period.

Venice, too, played a pivotal role in the Renaissance, with artists like Titian and Tintoretto leaving a lasting legacy. The Gallerie dell'Accademia in Venice houses a rich collection of Venetian Renaissance art, providing insight into the city's unique contribution to the movement. The Renaissance's emphasis on realism, perspective, and human emotion marked a departure from the more rigid and symbolic art of the Middle Ages, influencing countless artists and movements worldwide.

4.1.2 Modern Art and Contemporary Galleries

Italy also embraces modern and contemporary art, with vibrant galleries and museums that celebrate the country's ongoing contribution to the global art scene. The Peggy Guggenheim Collection in Venice features works by Picasso, Pollock, and Dalí, highlighting the innovative spirit of 20th-century art. This collection, housed in the Palazzo Venier dei Leoni, provides a stunning contrast to Venice's historical architecture, showcasing avant-garde masterpieces in a traditional setting.

In Milan, the Triennale Museum celebrates contemporary design and architecture, reflecting Italy's continued influence on modern aesthetics. The Museo del Novecento in Milan is dedicated to 20th-century art, offering a comprehensive overview of Italian and international modernism. These venues provide a dynamic contrast to Italy's classical art, illustrating the country's continuous contribution to artistic innovation.

Rome's MAXXI (National Museum of 21st Century Arts) and the MACRO (Museum of Contemporary Art of Rome) are also notable for their extensive collections of contemporary art. These institutions feature works by emerging and established artists, fostering an appreciation for the evolving landscape of global art. Italy's embrace of modern and contemporary art reflects its openness to new ideas and its enduring role as a cultural leader.

4.2 Festivals and Events

Italy's festivals and events offer immersive cultural experiences, celebrating the country's traditions, history, and community spirit. These events provide a vibrant insight into Italian life, from grand spectacles to intimate local gatherings. Each region has its own unique celebrations, showcasing the diverse cultural heritage of the country. Here are some of the most notable festivals and events that capture the essence of Italy.

4.2.1 Carnevale in Venice

One of the most famous festivals in Italy is Carnevale, particularly the celebration in Venice. Held annually before Lent, this event is characterized by elaborate masks, costumes, and festivities that fill the city's canals and squares. The tradition of mask-wearing dates back to the 13th century, creating an atmosphere of mystery and enchantment. The festival includes grand balls, parades, and street performances, with highlights such as the Flight of the Angel, where a performer descends from the bell tower of St. Mark's Basilica to the square below. Carnevale in Venice is a visual feast and offers visitors a chance to step into a world of fantasy and historical

tradition.

4.2.2 Palio di Siena

The Palio di Siena is another thrilling event, held twice a year in the Piazza del Campo in Siena. This historic horse race, dating back to the 16th century, features ten horses and riders representing different city districts (contrade). The race itself is a dramatic 90-second sprint around the piazza, but the event includes days of pageantry, processions in medieval costumes, and flag-throwing displays. The Palio reflects Siena's deep sense of tradition and community pride, offering visitors a unique and exhilarating glimpse into Italian cultural heritage. The intense rivalry and passionate support of each contrada create an electrifying atmosphere that captivates spectators.

4.2.3 Festa della Sensa in Venice

Another notable event in Venice is the Festa della Sensa, which commemorates the city's historical marriage to the sea. Held on Ascension Day, this festival dates back to the year 1000 and includes a symbolic wedding ceremony where the Doge of Venice would throw a ring into the sea. Today, the celebration features a grand procession of boats, historical reenactments, and various water sports. The Festa della Sensa is a beautiful blend of tradition and spectacle, celebrating Venice's maritime heritage and its deep connection to the sea.

4.2.4 Infiorata Festivals

The Infiorata festivals, held in various towns across Italy, are another charming celebration. During these festivals, the streets are decorated with intricate floral carpets made from petals, seeds, and other natural materials. The most famous Infiorata takes place in Spello and Genzano di Roma, where the streets are transformed into stunning works of art. These festivals usually coincide with religious celebrations like Corpus Christi, adding a spiritual dimension to the vibrant display of colors and creativity. Walking through these floral masterpieces is a sensory delight and a testament to the community's artistic talent and devotion.

4.2.5 Umbria Jazz Festival

Music lovers should not miss the Umbria Jazz Festival, one of the most important jazz festivals in the world. Held annually in Perugia, this festival attracts renowned international and Italian jazz musicians. Over ten days, the medieval city comes alive with performances in historic venues, open-air concerts, and jam sessions that continue late into the night. The festival offers a diverse program that includes traditional jazz, contemporary music, and experimental sounds. The Umbria Jazz Festival not only showcases incredible musical talent but also highlights the beauty and cultural richness of Perugia.

4.2.6 Sagra del Tartufo

Food festivals, or sagre, are an integral part of Italian culture, celebrating local culinary traditions and seasonal specialties. The Sagra del Tartufo, or Truffle Festival, held in regions like Alba and San Miniato, is a must-visit for food enthusiasts. These festivals celebrate the prized truffle with markets, tastings, and gourmet meals that highlight the unique flavors of this rare delicacy. Visitors can also participate in truffle hunts, guided by experts and trained dogs, providing a hands-on experience of this cherished tradition. The Sagra del Tartufo is a gastronomic adventure that offers a deeper appreciation of Italy's rich culinary heritage.

These festivals and events offer a vibrant and immersive experience of Italian culture, showcasing the country's love for tradition, celebration, and community. Whether you're dancing at Carnevale in Venice, cheering at the Palio di Siena, admiring floral art at the Infiorata, enjoying world-class jazz in Umbria, or savoring truffles in Alba, these celebrations provide unforgettable memories and a deeper connection to Italy's diverse and rich cultural tapestry.4.2.1 Carnevale in Venice

Carnevale in Venice is a world-famous event characterized by elaborate masks, costumes, and festivities. Held annually before Lent, this vibrant celebration fills the city's canals and squares with parades, masked balls, and performances. The tradition of mask-wearing dates back to the 13th century, originally allowing Venetians to conceal their identities and social differences during the festivities.

The grandeur of Carnevale is evident in the intricate costumes and masks, which are often handmade and passed down through generations. The atmosphere of mystery and enchantment permeates the city, transforming Venice into a living theater. Visitors can participate in public events or enjoy the spectacle as onlookers, experiencing the unique blend of history, culture, and entertainment that defines Carnevale.

4.2.2 Palio di Siena
The Palio di Siena is a thrilling horse race held twice a year in Siena's Piazza del Campo. Each race sees ten horses and riders, representing different city districts (contrade), competing in a fiercely contested event that lasts just 90 seconds. The race is preceded by days of pageantry, including parades in medieval costumes, flag-throwing displays, and the blessing of the horses in local churches.

The Palio is not just a race; it is a symbol of Siena's deep sense of tradition and community pride. The event dates back to the Middle Ages and is a culmination of centuries-old rivalries between the contrade. The intensity of the competition and the vibrant celebrations create a unique and exhilarating atmosphere.

For visitors, the Palio offers a glimpse into Italian cultural heritage, showcasing the city's historical roots and communal spirit. The sense of unity and rivalry, the elaborate rituals, and the sheer excitement of the race make it an unforgettable experience. The Palio reflects the passion and dedication of the Sienese people, highlighting the rich tapestry of Italian traditions.

In addition to these major events, Italy hosts numerous local festivals that celebrate everything from regional cuisine to religious traditions. The Festa della Repubblica (Republic Day) on June 2nd celebrates the birth of the Italian Republic with parades, concerts, and fireworks across the country. The Infiorata festivals, held in various towns, feature streets carpeted with intricate flower designs, showcasing the artistic creativity of local communities.

These festivals and events provide an immersive way to experience Italy's cultural treasures, offering insights into the country's rich traditions and vibrant community life. From the grand spectacle of Carnevale to the intense rivalry of the Palio, Italy's festivals capture the spirit of its people and the enduring beauty of its cultural heritage.

Chapter 5: Culinary Delights

5.1 Regional Italian Cuisine

Italy's culinary diversity reflects its regional variations, offering an array of flavors and dishes unique to each area. The distinct geographical, cultural, and historical influences of each region contribute to the richness and variety of Italian cuisine, making it a delightful journey for any food lover.

Northern Italian Specialties

In Northern Italy, the cuisine is characterized by its hearty and rich flavors. The regions of Piedmont, Lombardy, and Veneto are particularly notable for their culinary traditions.

Piedmont is famous for its use of truffles, particularly the white truffle from Alba, which adds an earthy and luxurious flavor to dishes. The region is also known for bagna càuda, a warm dip made from garlic, anchovies, olive oil, and butter, traditionally served with raw vegetables. Vitello tonnato (veal with tuna sauce) is another Piedmontese specialty, showcasing the region's unique flavor combinations.

Lombardy is home to Milan, where risotto alla Milanese (saffron risotto) and osso buco (braised veal shanks) are iconic dishes. The region's cuisine is rich in butter, cheese, and meats, reflecting its colder climate and agricultural heritage. Polenta, made from cornmeal, is a staple in Lombardy and often served with hearty stews or grilled meats.

Veneto is renowned for its rice dishes, especially risotto. Risotto al nero di seppia (risotto with cuttlefish ink) is a Venetian specialty, offering a unique and striking appearance. Baccalà mantecato (creamed cod) is another traditional dish, often served as an appetizer on crostini.

Central Italian Flavors

Central Italy, including Tuscany, Umbria, and Lazio, is known for its simple yet flavorful cuisine, focusing on high-quality ingredients and traditional cooking methods.

Tuscany is celebrated for its rustic and hearty dishes. Bistecca alla Fiorentina (Florentine steak), a thick, juicy steak typically from Chianina cattle, is a must-try. Ribollita, a Tuscan bread soup made with vegetables and beans, reflects the region's peasant roots. Pappa al pomodoro, another traditional Tuscan dish, is a thick tomato and bread soup, showcasing the region's love for simple, robust flavors.

Umbria, known as the "green heart of Italy," offers dishes that emphasize the use of local produce and game. Porchetta, a savory, herb-stuffed pork roast, is a popular dish, often enjoyed during festivals and special occasions. Strangozzi pasta, often served with black truffles or wild boar ragu, highlights Umbria's connection to its forests and countryside.

Lazio, home to Rome, boasts some of Italy's most beloved pasta dishes. Spaghetti alla carbonara, made with eggs, cheese, pancetta, and pepper, is a Roman classic. Cacio e pepe (cheese and pepper pasta) and amatriciana (pasta with tomato, guanciale, and pecorino cheese) are also staples of Roman cuisine. Supplì, deep-fried rice balls filled with cheese, are a popular street food in Rome.

Southern Italian Delicacies

Southern Italy's cuisine is characterized by bold flavors, fresh ingredients, and an abundance of seafood. The regions of Campania, Calabria, and Sicily each have distinct culinary identities.

Campania, where Naples is located, is the birthplace of pizza. Pizza Margherita, topped with tomatoes, mozzarella, and basil, is a classic that represents the colors of the Italian flag. The region is also known for sfogliatella, a layered pastry filled with ricotta and candied fruit, and pastiera, a traditional Easter cake made with ricotta and wheat berries. Spaghetti alle vongole (spaghetti with clams) is a quintessential Neapolitan seafood dish.

Calabria offers a cuisine rich in spicy and robust flavors. Nduja, a spreadable spicy pork sausage, is a Calabrian specialty that adds heat and depth to many dishes. Pasta alla 'nduja and cicoria e fagioli (chicory and beans) are staples of the region. Calabrian food often includes bergamot, a fragrant citrus fruit unique to the area, used in both savory and sweet dishes.

Sicily, with its unique blend of Mediterranean, Arab, and Norman influences, offers a diverse culinary landscape. Arancini, deep-fried rice balls filled with meat, cheese, or vegetables, are a popular snack. Caponata, a sweet and sour eggplant dish, reflects the island's love for bold flavors. Cannoli, crispy pastry tubes filled with sweet ricotta, are a beloved Sicilian dessert. The island's cuisine also features an abundance of seafood, such as pasta con le sarde (pasta with sardines) and pesce spada alla ghiotta (swordfish stew).

Sardinian and Alpine Influences

Beyond the mainland, Italy's islands and alpine regions add further depth to its culinary diversity. Sardinia is known for its distinctive dishes like porceddu (roast suckling pig) and culurgiones (stuffed pasta). The island's cheeses, particularly Pecorino Sardo, are renowned for their quality. Malloreddus, a type of small, ridged pasta, is often served with sausage and tomato sauce.

In the Aosta Valley and Trentino-Alto Adige, the cuisine is heavily influenced by neighboring France and Austria. Fontina cheese from the Aosta Valley is a key ingredient in fonduta, a rich cheese fondue. Canederli (bread dumplings) and speck (smoked ham) are staples in Trentino-Alto Adige, reflecting the region's alpine traditions.

Exploring Regional Markets and Festivals

To truly appreciate the diversity of Italian cuisine, visiting local markets and food festivals is essential. Markets like Mercato Centrale in Florence, La Vucciria in Palermo, and Campo de' Fiori in Rome offer a vibrant display of regional produce, meats, cheeses, and artisanal products. These markets are not only great places to buy ingredients but also provide an opportunity to observe the daily rhythms of Italian life and interact with local vendors.

Food festivals, or sagre, celebrate regional specialties and seasonal ingredients. The Sagra del Tartufo in Alba, the Sagra del Pesce in Camogli, and the Festa della Mozzarella in Paestum are just a few examples of festivals where visitors can indulge in local delicacies and experience the communal joy of Italian food culture.

Conclusion

Italy's regional cuisine is a testament to the country's rich cultural heritage and the diversity of its landscapes. From the hearty dishes of the north to the vibrant flavors of the south, each region offers unique culinary experiences that reflect its history, traditions, and local ingredients. Exploring Italy's regional cuisine is not just about tasting delicious food; it's about understanding the stories and traditions that have shaped these dishes over centuries. Whether you're savoring a simple plate of pasta in Rome, indulging in seafood in Sicily, or enjoying a rich risotto in Milan, Italian cuisine is a journey of discovery that delights the senses and enriches the soul.5.1.1 Northern Italian Specialties

Northern Italy is known for its rich, hearty dishes that often feature butter, cream, and cheese, reflecting the region's colder climate and agricultural abundance. In Lombardy, risotto alla Milanese, infused with saffron, is a creamy delight that perfectly exemplifies the region's penchant for luxurious flavors. This dish, often served with ossobuco (braised veal shanks), highlights the sophistication and depth of northern Italian cooking.

Piedmont, another northern region, is famous for its truffles, particularly the white truffle from Alba. These aromatic fungi are often shaved over pasta, risotto, and eggs, adding an earthy, intense flavor. The region is also known for robust dishes like bagna càuda, a warm dip made from garlic, anchovies, and olive oil, traditionally served with raw vegetables. Piedmont's cuisine is a reflection of its agricultural bounty and the meticulous craftsmanship of its food producers.

The Veneto region offers polenta, a versatile cornmeal dish that can be served creamy, grilled, or fried. Polenta pairs well with a variety of toppings, from rich meat stews to delicate seafood. Another Venetian specialty is baccalà mantecato, a creamy cod spread typically served on crostini. This dish, made from dried and salted cod, is a testament to Venice's maritime heritage and its ability to transform simple ingredients into culinary masterpieces.

Emilia-Romagna, often considered the culinary heart of Italy, is the birthplace of Parmigiano-Reggiano and Prosciutto di Parma. Traditional pasta dishes like tagliatelle al ragù (known outside Italy as Bolognese) and tortellini en brodo showcase the region's culinary excellence. Tagliatelle al ragù is a hearty pasta dish made with a slow-cooked meat sauce, while tortellini en brodo features delicate pasta filled with meat or cheese, served in a rich broth. Emilia-Romagna's cuisine is celebrated for its balance of flavors and the quality of its ingredients, making it a must-visit for any food enthusiast.

5.1.2 Southern Italian Flavors

Southern Italian cuisine is characterized by bold flavors and fresh ingredients, often reflecting the sunny climate and fertile land of the region. In Sicily, arancini, cannoli, and pasta alla Norma are iconic dishes that showcase the island's culinary heritage. Arancini are deep-fried rice balls filled with ragù, mozzarella, and peas, offering a satisfying crunch and savory flavor. Cannoli, crispy pastry tubes filled with sweet ricotta cheese, are a beloved Sicilian dessert, while pasta alla Norma features eggplant, tomatoes, and ricotta salata, embodying the island's love for simple, yet flavorful ingredients.

Calabria's cuisine is known for its spicy nduja sausage and hearty eggplant parmigiana. Nduja, a spreadable pork sausage with a fiery kick, is often used to add depth and heat to pasta dishes, pizzas, and sandwiches. Eggplant parmigiana, layers of fried eggplant, tomato sauce, and cheese, baked to perfection, is a comforting dish that highlights the region's agricultural bounty.

The Amalfi Coast offers limoncello and seafood dishes like spaghetti alle vongole. Limoncello, a bright and zesty lemon liqueur, is a refreshing digestif that captures the essence of the region's abundant lemon groves. Spaghetti alle vongole, made with fresh clams, garlic, white wine, and parsley, is a quintessential coastal dish that exemplifies the simplicity and freshness of southern Italian cuisine.

In Puglia, orecchiette pasta with broccoli rabe is a beloved dish, reflecting the region's agricultural bounty and Mediterranean influences. Orecchiette, meaning "little ears," is a small, round pasta that pairs perfectly with the slightly bitter greens and savory sausage often included in the dish. Puglia's cuisine is known for its focus on fresh, local ingredients and its celebration of simple, rustic flavors.

5.2 Cooking Classes and Food Tours

Immersing oneself in Italy's culinary culture is a must for food enthusiasts, with cooking classes and food tours providing hands-on experiences that deepen the appreciation for Italian cuisine.

5.2.1 Learning to Cook Like an Italian

Cooking classes across Italy teach traditional techniques and recipes, from making fresh pasta to crafting authentic pizzas. These classes are often held in picturesque settings, allowing participants to enjoy the beauty of the Italian countryside or the charm of historic cities while learning to cook. In Tuscany, participants can learn to prepare a full Italian meal, including antipasti, pasta, and dessert. These classes often take place in rustic farmhouses or elegant villas, providing a truly immersive experience.

In cities like Bologna, renowned for its culinary heritage, cooking classes offer insights into regional specialties and the art of Italian cooking. Participants might learn to make tortellini, tagliatelle, or Bolognese sauce, guided by experienced chefs who share their knowledge and passion for local cuisine. These classes often include trips to local markets, where participants can select fresh ingredients and learn about the importance of seasonality and quality in Italian cooking.

Rome offers numerous cooking classes where participants can learn to make classic Roman dishes such as carbonara, amatriciana, and cacio e pepe. These classes provide a deeper understanding of the simplicity and elegance of Roman cuisine, emphasizing the use of high-quality ingredients and traditional techniques.

In southern Italy, cooking classes often focus on seafood and fresh vegetables, reflecting the region's Mediterranean influences. Participants can learn to make dishes such as Sicilian caponata, Neapolitan pizza, or Calabrian swordfish. These classes provide a hands-on experience of southern Italian cooking, highlighting the bold flavors and vibrant colors that characterize the region's cuisine.

5.2.2 Best Food Markets and Street Food
Exploring Italy's food markets and street food scenes offers a taste of local life and culinary traditions. The Mercato Centrale in Florence and the Mercato di Sant'Ambrogio are ideal for sampling local cheeses, cured meats, and fresh produce. These bustling markets provide a sensory overload of sights, smells, and flavors, allowing visitors to experience the vibrant energy of Italian food culture.

In Palermo, Sicily, street food markets like Ballarò and Vucciria offer arancini, panelle, and sfincione. Arancini, deep-fried rice balls filled with ragù, mozzarella, and peas, are a beloved Sicilian snack. Panelle, chickpea fritters, and sfincione, a thick, spongy pizza topped with tomatoes, onions, and anchovies, are other popular street foods that reflect Palermo's rich culinary heritage.

Rome's Testaccio Market is famous for its diverse food stalls, providing everything from fresh pasta to artisanal gelato. Visitors can sample traditional Roman dishes such as supplì (rice croquettes), porchetta (roast pork), and carciofi alla giudia (Jewish-style artichokes). The market is also a great place to discover new flavors and ingredients, with vendors offering a wide range of local and seasonal products.

In Naples, street food is a way of life, with vendors offering everything from pizza al portafoglio (folded pizza) to sfogliatella (a shell-shaped pastry filled with sweet ricotta). The city's vibrant street food scene is a testament to its rich culinary traditions and the creativity of its food artisans.

Exploring these vibrant markets and street food vendors provides an authentic taste of Italy's culinary landscape, allowing visitors to experience the diversity and richness of Italian cuisine in a casual, yet deeply satisfying way. Whether sampling freshly made pasta in Florence, savoring street food in Palermo, or enjoying a cooking class in Tuscany, these experiences offer a deeper connection to Italy's food culture and the people who bring it to life.

Chapter 6: Family-Friendly Travel
Italy is a fantastic destination for families, offering a rich blend of cultural experiences and kid-friendly activities. From interactive museums to outdoor adventures, Italy ensures that visitors of all ages can have an enjoyable and enriching experience. The country's diverse regions provide a variety of experiences that cater to children's interests and curiosity, making it an ideal destination for family vacations.

6.1 Activities for Kids

6.1.1 Interactive Museums and Workshops
Interactive museums and workshops across Italy make learning fun for children. In Rome, **Explora, the Children's Museum**, is designed specifically for kids, featuring hands-on exhibits that cover a range of topics from science and technology to art and history. Kids can engage in role-playing, experiment with interactive displays, and participate in workshops tailored to their age group. The museum's layout and activities are crafted to stimulate curiosity and creativity, ensuring a memorable visit for young minds.

In Florence, the **Leonardo da Vinci Museum** offers an engaging way to learn about the genius of Leonardo. The museum features interactive exhibits and life-size models of his inventions, allowing children to explore Leonardo's contributions to art and science. Similarly, the **Museo Galileo** in Florence provides hands-on exhibits related to the history of science, making it an exciting destination for curious young minds. These museums encourage children to think critically and creatively, enhancing their understanding of historical and scientific concepts through engaging activities.

Venice offers the **Peggy Guggenheim Collection**, which hosts family-oriented tours and workshops. These programs help children appreciate modern art through interactive activities and storytelling. The museum's beautiful setting along the Grand Canal adds to the experience, making art accessible and enjoyable for young visitors. Additionally, the **Città della Scienza** in Naples is a science museum that combines fun and education with interactive exhibits and live demonstrations. The museum's focus on hands-on learning makes it a popular attraction for families, providing a blend of entertainment and education.

6.1.2 Amusement Parks and Outdoor Adventures
Italy boasts several amusement parks and outdoor activities that are perfect for families. **Gardaland**, located near Lake Garda, is Italy's largest amusement park, offering a variety of rides and attractions for all ages. From thrilling roller coasters to gentle carousels and themed areas like Peppa Pig Land, Gardaland ensures a fun-filled day for the whole family. The park's diverse attractions cater to different age groups and interests, making it a versatile destination for family entertainment.

In the Emilia-Romagna region, **Mirabilandia** is another popular amusement park featuring water rides, roller coasters, and live shows. The park's Dinoland section is particularly appealing to young dinosaur enthusiasts, while the water park area provides a refreshing escape during the summer months. Mirabilandia's extensive range of attractions ensures that there is something for everyone, from adrenaline-pumping rides to family-friendly shows.

For outdoor adventures, families can explore the beautiful Italian countryside through activities like hiking and biking. The **Dolomites** in northern Italy offer numerous family-friendly trails with breathtaking scenery. These trails are suitable for various skill levels, allowing families to enjoy the natural beauty of the region at their own pace. In Tuscany, **agriturismo** stays provide a chance to experience rural life, with opportunities for horseback riding, farm tours, and cooking classes. These stays offer an immersive experience, allowing families to connect with nature and learn about sustainable farming practices.

The **Via Francigena**, an ancient pilgrimage route, offers a gentle hiking experience suitable for families, winding through picturesque villages and scenic landscapes. This historical trail provides an opportunity for families to explore Italy's countryside while enjoying the serenity and beauty of rural areas. Whether cycling through vineyards or hiking in national parks, Italy's outdoor adventures provide endless opportunities for family fun and bonding.

6.2 Tips for Traveling with Children

6.2.1 Packing Essentials

Traveling with children requires careful planning and packing. Essential items include travel documents, medications, and comfort items like favorite toys or blankets. Packing snacks and water bottles is crucial for keeping kids energized and hydrated during long travel days. Bringing a lightweight stroller or baby carrier can be helpful for navigating Italy's cobblestone streets and crowded tourist sites. Ensuring that you have all necessary documents and health items can prevent potential issues during your trip.

Comfortable clothing and shoes are a must, as exploring Italy often involves a lot of walking. Sunscreen, hats, and sunglasses are essential for protection against the Mediterranean sun. For younger children, packing a change of clothes and diapers is important. Additionally, a small first-aid kit with band-aids, antiseptic wipes, and any necessary medications is always useful. Being prepared with these essentials can make your travels smoother and more enjoyable for everyone.

When packing, consider the weather and the types of activities you will be doing. Italy's climate can vary significantly by region and season, so having layers and appropriate gear for different conditions is important. Also, think about the cultural norms and dress codes, especially when visiting religious sites. Ensuring that your family is comfortable and prepared for various scenarios will help you make the most of your trip.

6.2.2 Keeping Kids Engaged and Entertained

Keeping children engaged and entertained during a trip can make the experience more enjoyable for everyone. Planning activities that cater to their interests is key. Involve them in the trip planning process by letting them choose some attractions or activities. Interactive and educational experiences, such as museum scavenger hunts or cooking classes, can be both fun and informative. These activities not only keep children entertained but also help them learn and connect with the local culture.

On travel days, keeping kids entertained is crucial. Pack a bag with books, coloring supplies, puzzles, and travel-sized games. Electronic devices with headphones and pre-downloaded movies or educational apps can also be lifesavers during long flights or train rides. Encouraging kids to keep a travel journal or scrapbook can help them document their experiences and stay engaged with their surroundings. These activities provide a creative outlet and help children remember and reflect on their adventures.

In restaurants, choosing places with child-friendly menus and bringing small toys or activities can make dining out more pleasant. Taking breaks in parks or open spaces allows children to burn off energy and can be a great way to relax and enjoy the local scenery. Italy has many beautiful public spaces where families can unwind and play, from urban parks to countryside meadows.

Remembering to maintain a flexible schedule, allowing for downtime and spontaneous fun, ensures a balanced and enjoyable trip for the entire family. Sometimes the best experiences come from unplanned moments, so being open to changes and going with the flow can enhance your travels. Creating a balance between structured activities and free time helps keep everyone happy and relaxed.

Additionally, engaging with locals can enrich your family's experience. Italians are generally welcoming and love children, so don't hesitate to strike up conversations and seek recommendations for family-friendly activities and restaurants. Learning a few basic Italian phrases can also help children feel more connected and confident during their trip.

In summary, Italy offers a wealth of family-friendly activities and experiences that cater to all ages. By planning ahead, packing thoughtfully, and keeping children engaged, families can create lasting memories while exploring this beautiful and culturally rich country. From interactive museums and outdoor adventures to delicious food and welcoming locals, Italy is an ideal destination for family travel.

Chapter 7: Practical Travel Advice

7.1 Getting Around Italy

7.1.1 Public Transportation: Trains, Buses, and Ferries

Italy boasts an extensive and efficient public transportation system, making it easy for travelers to navigate the country. The train network, operated primarily by Trenitalia and Italo, connects major cities and towns, offering high-speed, regional, and local services. High-speed trains like the Frecciarossa and Italo trains link cities such as Rome, Florence, Milan, and Venice, significantly reducing travel time and providing a comfortable and scenic journey. These trains are known for their punctuality, cleanliness, and comfort, making them a preferred mode of transport for many tourists and locals alike.

Buses are another viable option, particularly for reaching destinations not serviced by trains. Companies like FlixBus and local operators offer routes that connect smaller towns and rural areas to larger cities. Bus travel is generally affordable, and the extensive network ensures that even remote locations are accessible. Buses often provide amenities such as free Wi-Fi, air conditioning, and onboard restrooms, making longer journeys more comfortable. Additionally, bus stations are usually centrally located, providing convenient access to city centers and major attractions.

Ferries are essential for exploring Italy's coastal regions and islands. Companies like Moby Lines, Tirrenia, and Grandi Navi Veloci operate services between the mainland and islands such as Sicily, Sardinia, and the Aeolian Islands. Ferries also connect popular coastal towns, offering a leisurely way to travel while enjoying picturesque views of the Mediterranean. Ferries vary in size and amenities, with some offering comfortable seating, dining options, and even cabins for overnight journeys. The ferry system is particularly useful for reaching destinations like Capri, Ischia, and Elba, where direct land routes are unavailable.

7.1.2 Renting a Car: Pros and Cons

Renting a car in Italy provides the flexibility to explore at your own pace, especially in regions where public transportation is limited. It allows for spontaneous detours and the convenience of traveling on your own schedule. Popular car rental companies such as Hertz, Avis, and Europcar offer a range of vehicles and rental options. Having a car can be particularly advantageous when exploring rural areas, the countryside, or coastal regions where public transportation options may be sparse.

However, there are also cons to consider. Driving in Italy can be challenging due to narrow streets, aggressive driving styles, and limited parking in cities. Urban areas, especially historic city centers, can be difficult to navigate due to the intricate street layouts and pedestrian zones. Additionally, many historic city centers have ZTL (Zona a Traffico Limitato) zones, which restrict access to vehicles without permits, and fines can be issued for violations. It is crucial to be aware of these zones to avoid hefty fines. Fuel costs and tolls on highways (autostrade) can add to travel expenses, making car rental potentially more expensive than public transportation. Before deciding to rent a car, it's important to weigh these factors and consider the specific needs of your trip. For instance, a car might be more useful for exploring Tuscany's vineyards or the Amalfi Coast's scenic drives than for navigating Rome's bustling streets.

7.2 Staying Safe and Healthy

7.2.1 Safety Tips for Tourists

Italy is generally a safe country for tourists, but taking common-sense precautions is essential. Pickpocketing can be an issue in crowded areas, so keep valuables secure and be aware of your surroundings. Use money belts or cross-body bags that zip securely, and avoid displaying expensive items. It's advisable to keep photocopies of important documents like passports and insurance policies in a separate location from the originals.

In busy tourist spots, be cautious of scams and overly friendly strangers. Always verify the authenticity of tour guides and services. Using reputable tour companies and booking in advance can help avoid potential scams. Be aware of your belongings in public transportation and avoid leaving bags unattended. Additionally, it's wise to familiarize yourself with common tourist scams and how to avoid them.

When traveling at night, stick to well-lit areas and avoid isolated streets. Trust your instincts and seek help from local authorities or your accommodation if you feel unsafe. Learning a few basic Italian phrases can also be helpful in case of emergencies. Phrases like "Aiuto!" (Help!), "Dov'è il bagno?" (Where is the bathroom?), and "Chiamate un dottore" (Call a doctor) can be particularly useful.

7.2.2 Health and Travel Insurance

Having comprehensive health and travel insurance is crucial when visiting Italy. Medical care is available throughout the country, but insurance ensures that you can access private facilities if necessary and covers unexpected medical expenses. Check that your policy includes coverage for medical emergencies, trip cancellations, lost luggage, and other travel-related issues. Travel insurance provides peace of mind and financial protection, ensuring that you are covered in case of unforeseen circumstances.

Carry a copy of your insurance policy and emergency contact numbers. In case of minor health issues, pharmacies (farmacie) are widely available and can provide over-the-counter medications and advice. Pharmacists in Italy are well-trained and can often assist with minor ailments. Pharmacies are typically marked with a green cross and are usually open during regular business hours, with some offering 24-hour service in larger cities.

For emergencies, dial 112, the European emergency number. Italy also has a robust healthcare system, and public hospitals (ospedali) provide quality care. However, having travel insurance ensures peace of mind and financial protection during your trip. It's also advisable to know the locations of nearby hospitals and clinics in case of serious health issues.

Additionally, staying healthy while traveling involves being mindful of food and water safety. Italy's tap water is generally safe to drink, but bottled water is widely available if preferred. Enjoying the local cuisine is a highlight of any trip to Italy, but it's wise to ensure that food is prepared and served in hygienic conditions, especially when eating street food or at less formal establishments.

By following these practical tips and advice, you can navigate Italy smoothly, stay safe, and enjoy a stress-free travel experience. Whether using public transportation, renting a car, or exploring on foot, being prepared and aware of your surroundings will enhance your journey through this beautiful and culturally rich country. Italy's welcoming atmosphere, combined with these practical considerations, ensures a memorable and enjoyable trip for all travelers.

Chapter 8: Accommodation Options

8.1 Hotels and Resorts

8.1.1 Best Luxury Stays

Italy offers an array of luxurious hotels and resorts, providing exceptional comfort, service, and amenities. These accommodations are not just places to stay; they are experiences in themselves, offering unique touches and lavish surroundings that make your visit unforgettable.

In Rome, the Hotel Hassler, located at the top of the Spanish Steps, offers breathtaking views, elegant rooms, and world-class dining. Its rooftop restaurant, Imàgo, provides a panoramic view of the city and a Michelin-starred menu. Another notable mention is the St. Regis Rome, known for its opulent decor and personalized service. This hotel combines historical elegance with modern luxury, featuring beautifully appointed rooms and a butler service that caters to your every need.

In Venice, the Belmond Hotel Cipriani offers a blend of historic charm and modern luxury, with stunning views of the lagoon and the Doge's Palace. This iconic hotel is accessible by a private boat and offers an array of amenities including a swimming pool, exquisite dining options, and lush gardens. The Gritti Palace, a Marriott Luxury Collection Hotel, provides an intimate atmosphere with its beautifully restored interiors and prime location on the Grand Canal. This hotel is famed for its luxurious rooms, each uniquely decorated with antiques and fine fabrics, and its culinary excellence.

The Amalfi Coast features the renowned Hotel Santa Caterina, perched on a cliff with panoramic sea views and a private beach. This family-run hotel combines Mediterranean elegance with exceptional service. For a tranquil escape, the Rosewood Castiglion del Bosco in Tuscany offers a luxurious stay amidst rolling vineyards. This resort features a spa, golf course, and exquisite dining experiences, all set in a historic estate that dates back to the 17th century.

8.1.2 Budget-Friendly Accommodations
Travelers on a budget will find numerous affordable accommodation options without compromising on comfort or location. In major cities like Rome, Florence, and Milan, budget hotels and hostels offer convenient access to key attractions.

The Generator Hostel in Rome provides stylish dorms and private rooms, along with a lively social atmosphere. This hostel is located near Termini Station, making it a convenient base for exploring the city. Florence's Hotel Alessandra offers cozy rooms in a historic building near the Ponte Vecchio, providing excellent value for money. Its central location allows guests to easily explore the Uffizi Gallery, the Duomo, and other major sights.

In Venice, the We Crociferi hostel, housed in a former convent, combines affordability with unique historical charm and modern amenities. This hostel offers private rooms and dormitories, a spacious courtyard, and a bar, all within walking distance of Venice's top attractions.

For countryside stays, many agriturismos (farm stays) offer budget-friendly rates. These accommodations, often family-run, provide comfortable rooms, hearty meals, and the opportunity to experience rural Italian life. Agriturismos are especially popular in regions like Tuscany, Umbria, and Puglia. Staying at an agriturismo allows visitors to enjoy the beauty of the Italian countryside while participating in activities like olive picking, cheese making, and wine tasting.

8.2 Unique Stays

8.2.1 Agriturismos and Farm Stays

Agriturismos offer a unique and immersive accommodation experience, allowing travelers to stay on working farms. These stays provide insight into local agricultural practices and the chance to enjoy fresh, farm-to-table cuisine.

In Tuscany, Agriturismo Il Rigo offers rustic charm and stunning views of the Val d'Orcia. Guests can participate in cooking classes, wine tastings, and farm activities, making it a perfect destination for those looking to connect with nature and Italian traditions. The farm produces its own olive oil, wine, and other products, giving guests a true taste of the region's bounty.

In Sicily, Agriturismo Case Brizza provides a tranquil retreat with beautifully restored stone buildings, olive groves, and organic produce. The farm-to-table dining experience here showcases the best of Sicilian cuisine, with meals prepared using ingredients grown on the farm. Guests can explore the surrounding countryside, relax by the pool, or take part in cooking classes and guided tours of the area.

In the Piedmont region, Agriturismo Cascina Barac offers comfortable accommodations amidst vineyards, with wine tastings and vineyard tours. This agriturismo is located in the heart of the Langhe wine region, famous for its Barolo and Barbaresco wines. Guests can learn about the winemaking process, explore the vineyards, and enjoy the beautiful scenery of the rolling hills.

8.2.2 Boutique Hotels and B&Bs

Italy's boutique hotels and B&Bs offer personalized service and distinctive character, often housed in historic buildings. These accommodations provide a more intimate and unique experience compared to larger hotels, blending modern comforts with traditional charm. Here are some of the best examples of boutique hotels and B&Bs across Italy that cater to travelers seeking an authentic and memorable stay.

Florence

In Florence, AdAstra offers elegant rooms and suites with eclectic decor, set within the largest private garden in Europe. Each room is uniquely decorated, providing a blend of contemporary style and historical elements. The tranquil garden is an oasis in the bustling city, perfect for relaxing after a day of sightseeing. The hotel's personalized service ensures that guests feel at home, with attentive staff ready to offer recommendations and assistance. The location in the Oltrarno district, known for its artisan workshops and bohemian vibe, adds to the hotel's appeal, allowing guests to explore a less touristy side of Florence.

Another notable boutique hotel in Florence is J.K. Place Firenze. Situated near Piazza Santa Maria Novella, this hotel combines luxurious furnishings with a homely atmosphere. The rooftop terrace offers stunning views of the city, making it an ideal spot for breakfast or an evening drink. The rooms are stylishly decorated with a mix of classic and modern design, and the hotel's central location makes it a perfect base for exploring Florence's cultural and historical sites.

Rome

In Rome, The Fifteen Keys Hotel is located in the trendy Monti district, offering chic rooms with modern amenities and a welcoming atmosphere. Its central location provides easy access to major attractions, making it an ideal base for exploring the city. The hotel's personalized service and stylish design make it a favorite among travelers seeking a boutique experience. Guests can enjoy a cozy lounge area and a delightful breakfast in the courtyard, adding to the hotel's charm.

Another excellent choice in Rome is Casa Montani, a small luxury B&B located near Piazza del Popolo. This B&B offers elegantly furnished rooms with a mix of antique and contemporary decor. The personalized service includes a customized breakfast served in-room, ensuring a comfortable and unique experience. The proximity to major attractions such as the Spanish Steps and Villa Borghese makes it a convenient and stylish option for visitors.

Venice

Venice's Ca Maria Adele combines luxurious accommodations with a romantic setting near the Salute Church. Each room is uniquely designed, reflecting Venetian opulence and charm. The attentive service and intimate ambiance make it a favorite for couples. The hotel's prime location offers stunning views of the Grand Canal and easy access to Venice's major sights. Guests can enjoy a private breakfast in their room or in one of the cozy lounges, adding to the sense of exclusivity and romance.

Another standout in Venice is Hotel Moresco, located in the Dorsoduro district. This boutique hotel features elegantly decorated rooms with a mix of modern and traditional Venetian styles. The hotel's garden and lounge areas provide peaceful retreats after a day of exploring the city. The friendly and helpful staff go out of their way to ensure guests have a memorable stay, offering personalized recommendations and services.

Countryside Escapes

For a countryside escape, B&B La Locanda del Capitano in Umbria offers a cozy and intimate stay with beautifully decorated rooms and a renowned restaurant serving local specialties. The friendly hosts provide personalized recommendations for exploring the region, ensuring that guests have a memorable and enjoyable stay. The B&B's location in the medieval village of Montone adds to its charm, offering a glimpse into the region's history and culture. The restaurant is a highlight, featuring dishes made with locally sourced ingredients and reflecting the rich culinary traditions of Umbria.

In Tuscany, Relais Borgo Santo Pietro offers a luxurious retreat in a restored 13th-century villa. The property features beautifully landscaped gardens, a spa, and a Michelin-starred restaurant. Guests can enjoy activities such as cooking classes, wine tastings, and truffle hunting, making it a perfect destination for those looking to immerse themselves in the Tuscan lifestyle. The rooms and suites are exquisitely decorated, combining rustic charm with modern luxury.

Coastal Retreats

On the Amalfi Coast, Casa Angelina offers a contemporary boutique hotel experience with breathtaking views of the Mediterranean Sea. Located in Praiano, this hotel features minimalist design and modern amenities, providing a serene and stylish retreat. The rooftop terrace, infinity pool, and gourmet restaurant make it an ideal choice for those seeking luxury and tranquility.

In Sicily, Monaci delle Terre Nere provides a unique boutique hotel experience on the slopes of Mount Etna. This eco-friendly estate offers luxurious accommodations in restored farm buildings surrounded by vineyards and orchards. Guests can explore the estate's organic farm, enjoy wine tastings, and savor Sicilian cuisine at the on-site restaurant. The combination of natural beauty, sustainable practices, and elegant design makes it a standout choice for travelers.

Conclusion

These unique stays provide a memorable and enriching experience, allowing travelers to immerse themselves in Italy's diverse landscapes and cultures. Whether opting for a luxury hotel, a budget-friendly hostel, an agriturismo, or a boutique B&B, Italy offers accommodations to suit every taste and budget. Each type of accommodation provides its own unique charm and opportunities for exploring the beauty and culture of Italy, ensuring that every stay is a special and unforgettable experience. From the heart of historic cities to the serene countryside and stunning coastlines, Italy's boutique hotels and B&Bs offer the perfect blend of comfort, luxury, and personalized service.

Chapter 9: Itineraries and Day Trips

9.1 Suggested Itineraries

9.1.1 One Week in Italy: A Comprehensive Tour

A one-week itinerary offers a glimpse into Italy's rich cultural and historical tapestry, focusing on its most iconic cities. Begin your adventure in Rome, the Eternal City, where you'll spend two days immersing yourself in the grandeur of ancient history. Start with the Colosseum, an architectural marvel and symbol of the Roman Empire's might. Nearby, explore the Roman Forum, the center of ancient Roman public life, where you can walk among the ruins of temples, basilicas, and public spaces.

No visit to Rome is complete without experiencing the Vatican City. Marvel at the grandeur of St. Peter's Basilica, and be awed by Michelangelo's masterpiece on the ceiling of the Sistine Chapel. Take a leisurely stroll through the historic center of Rome, visiting the Trevi Fountain, where legend has it that throwing a coin into the water ensures your return to the city, and the Spanish Steps, a popular meeting place offering stunning views of the surrounding area.

Next, take a high-speed train to Florence, the cradle of the Renaissance, for two days. Visit the Uffizi Gallery to see works by Botticelli and Leonardo da Vinci, and marvel at Michelangelo's David in the Accademia Gallery. Wander through the Piazza del Duomo to see the Florence Cathedral and its impressive dome designed by Brunelleschi. Florence is a city of art and beauty, where every corner tells a story of creativity and innovation.

From Florence, embark on a day trip to Pisa to see the famous Leaning Tower. This iconic structure, part of the cathedral complex known as the Piazza dei Miracoli, is a must-see. Climbing the tower offers a unique perspective of the city and the surrounding countryside.

Conclude your week with two days in Venice. Explore St. Mark's Basilica, an architectural wonder adorned with stunning mosaics. Visit the Doge's Palace, a symbol of Venice's political and cultural history. Take a romantic gondola ride along the Grand Canal, Venice's main waterway, and get lost in the maze-like streets and hidden squares. Venice's charm lies in its unique blend of history, art, and serene beauty.

9.1.2 Two-Week Adventure: From North to South
A two-week adventure allows for a deeper exploration of Italy's diverse regions, from the northern Alps to the southern coasts. Begin in Milan, Italy's fashion capital, where you can visit the Duomo, a stunning example of Gothic architecture, and the Sforza Castle, which houses several museums and art collections. Don't miss Leonardo da Vinci's Last Supper at the Convent of Santa Maria delle Grazie.

Spend two days in Milan before heading to the lakes, with a visit to Lake Como, known for its scenic beauty and charming towns like Bellagio and Varenna. Enjoy a boat ride on the lake, surrounded by mountains and elegant villas, and explore the quaint streets of these lakeside towns.

From Lake Como, travel to Venice for two days to experience its unique waterways and historic sites. Next, head to Florence for three days, taking time to explore not just the city's art and architecture but also the surrounding Tuscan countryside. Visit towns like Siena, with its stunning Gothic cathedral and the famous Piazza del Campo, and San Gimignano, known for its medieval towers and beautiful frescoes.

After Florence, make your way to Rome for three days of in-depth exploration. Include day trips to nearby sites such as Ostia Antica, the ancient port of Rome, and Tivoli's Villa d'Este, a Renaissance villa famous for its terraced hillside Italian Renaissance garden and fountain displays.

Then, travel south to Naples for two days, using it as a base to visit Pompeii and Mount Vesuvius. Pompeii, an ancient city buried by the eruption of Mount Vesuvius in 79 AD, offers a fascinating glimpse into Roman life with its well-preserved ruins.

Conclude your journey on the Amalfi Coast, spending two days in towns like Positano, Amalfi, and Ravello. Enjoy the stunning coastal views, delicious cuisine, and the laid-back atmosphere. Positano's cliffside houses and boutique shops provide a picturesque setting, while Amalfi's historic cathedral and harbor offer rich cultural experiences. Ravello, perched high above the coast, is known for its beautiful gardens and panoramic views, particularly from Villa Rufolo and Villa Cimbrone.

9.2 Best Day Trips
9.2.1 Exploring the Tuscan Countryside
The Tuscan countryside is a picturesque landscape of rolling hills, vineyards, and charming medieval towns, perfect for a day trip from Florence or Siena. Visit the town of San Gimignano, known for its medieval towers and beautiful frescoes. Stroll

through its cobblestone streets, enjoy local wines, and savor Tuscan cuisine in a traditional trattoria. San Gimignano's skyline, dotted with towers, is often referred to as the "Medieval Manhattan."

Another must-see is the town of Siena, with its stunning Gothic cathedral and the famous Piazza del Campo, where the Palio horse race takes place twice a year. The Palio is a colorful, chaotic, and deeply traditional event that dates back centuries. The Chianti region, renowned for its wine, offers numerous wineries where you can tour vineyards, learn about wine production, and enjoy tastings. Exploring the Chianti region by car or bike is a delightful way to experience the Tuscan countryside, with its scenic routes and quaint villages.

9.2.2 Discovering the Amalfi Coast
A day trip to the Amalfi Coast from Naples or Sorrento offers breathtaking views, charming villages, and the azure sea. Begin in Positano, a cliffside village with colorful houses, boutique shops, and inviting beaches. Wander through its narrow streets and enjoy the scenic vistas. Positano is famous for its vertical landscape, where steps replace streets in many parts of the village.

Next, visit Amalfi, with its historic cathedral and picturesque harbor. The Amalfi Cathedral, dedicated to Saint Andrew, is a stunning example of medieval architecture with its striped facade and magnificent cloister. From Amalfi, take a drive up to Ravello, known for its stunning gardens and panoramic views of the coastline. The Villa Rufolo and Villa Cimbrone offer beautiful gardens and terraces overlooking the sea, providing a tranquil retreat.

For those interested in history, a visit to Pompeii or Herculaneum, ancient cities buried by the eruption of Mount Vesuvius, provides a fascinating glimpse into Roman life. These well-preserved archaeological sites are easily accessible from the Amalfi Coast and offer an enriching addition to your coastal adventure. Walking through the streets of Pompeii, you can see the remains of homes, shops, and public buildings, frozen in time by the volcanic ash.

These itineraries and day trips showcase the best of Italy, from its cultural capitals to its scenic landscapes, ensuring a memorable and diverse travel experience. Whether you have one week or two, Italy's rich history, stunning scenery, and vibrant culture offer endless opportunities for exploration and enjoyment. By planning your trip with these itineraries, you can experience the essence of Italy, making your visit both fulfilling and unforgettable.

Chapter 10: Insider Tips and Resources

10.1 Local Insights and Recommendations

10.1.1 Avoiding Tourist Traps

Italy, with its rich history and vibrant culture, attracts millions of tourists each year. While popular destinations like Rome, Venice, and Florence are must-sees, they can also be crowded and expensive. To avoid tourist traps and have a more authentic experience, consider the following tips:

Research and Plan Ahead: Prioritize what you want to see and do. Booking tickets online for major attractions like the Colosseum, Uffizi Gallery, and St. Mark's Basilica can save time and avoid long lines. Planning ahead allows you to maximize your time and focus on enjoying your visit rather than standing in queues. Additionally, many sites offer guided tours that can provide deeper insights into the history and significance of the attractions.

Explore Lesser-Known Neighborhoods: In Rome, for example, venture beyond the historic center to neighborhoods like Trastevere, Testaccio, or Monti, where you can enjoy authentic cuisine and vibrant local culture. Trastevere is known for its bohemian atmosphere, charming streets, and vibrant nightlife. Testaccio, traditionally a working-class district, has evolved into a foodie haven with markets, bakeries, and traditional trattorias. Monti, with its eclectic boutiques and artsy vibe, offers a more relaxed pace compared to the bustling city center.

Dine Like a Local: Avoid restaurants with tourist menus or those located too close to major attractions. Instead, look for trattorias and osterias frequented by locals. Inquire with your hotel staff or use apps like TripAdvisor and Yelp to find highly recommended eateries. Authentic local dining spots often offer better quality food at reasonable prices, and provide a genuine taste of regional specialties. Trying local dishes and regional wines can significantly enhance your culinary experience in Italy.

Be Wary of Overpriced Souvenirs: Tourist-heavy areas often inflate prices on souvenirs. For unique and affordable gifts, visit local markets, artisanal shops, and smaller towns known for their crafts. Handmade ceramics from Deruta, leather goods from Florence, and glass from Murano are examples of authentic Italian crafts that make wonderful souvenirs. Shopping in local markets not only supports small businesses but also offers the opportunity to find one-of-a-kind items.

Stay in Smaller Towns: Consider basing yourself in smaller towns or villages instead of large cities. Places like Lucca, Assisi, and Orvieto offer rich historical experiences, charming atmospheres, and fewer crowds. From these towns, you can easily take day trips to nearby major attractions, enjoying the best of both worlds.

Use Public Transportation Wisely: While taxis and ride-shares can be convenient, using public transportation like buses and trains can save money and provide a more local experience. Italy's train network is extensive and efficient, connecting major cities and smaller towns. Using regional trains can also offer scenic views of the countryside and an opportunity to mingle with locals.

Avoid Peak Tourist Seasons: If possible, plan your visit during the shoulder seasons of spring (April to June) and fall (September to October). These times generally have milder weather and fewer tourists, allowing for a more pleasant and relaxed experience. Visiting popular attractions early in the morning or late in the afternoon can also help you avoid the busiest times of the day.

10.1.2 Discovering Authentic Experiences

To truly experience Italy's rich culture and heritage, seek out authentic experiences that go beyond the typical tourist itinerary:

Participate in Local Festivals: Attending local festivals is a fantastic way to immerse yourself in Italian culture. Events like the Carnival of Venice, the Palio di Siena, and various regional food festivals offer unique insights into local traditions. The Carnival of Venice, with its elaborate masks and costumes, provides a colorful and festive atmosphere, while the Palio di Siena, a historic horse race, offers a thrilling glimpse into local rivalries and community pride. Food festivals, such as those celebrating truffles in Alba or wine in Chianti, allow you to indulge in local specialties and learn about regional culinary traditions.

Take a Cooking Class: Learning to cook Italian dishes with a local chef can be a memorable experience. Classes often include a visit to a local market, providing an opportunity to learn about regional ingredients and culinary techniques. Whether making pasta in Bologna, pizza in Naples, or risotto in Milan, these classes offer hands-on experience and delicious results. Many cooking schools also provide recipes and tips that you can take home, allowing you to recreate Italian dishes long after your trip.

Visit Family-Owned Wineries and Farms: Italy is famous for its wine and olive oil. Touring family-owned wineries and farms allows you to see the production process and taste the products while supporting local businesses. Regions like Tuscany, Piedmont, and Sicily offer a wealth of options for wine tours and tastings. Visiting these establishments provides insight into traditional methods and the opportunity to sample high-quality products in picturesque settings.

Explore Historical Sites Off the Beaten Path: While iconic landmarks are essential, exploring lesser-known historical sites can be equally rewarding. Places like the Etruscan tombs in Tarquinia, the Roman amphitheater in Verona, and the medieval villages of Abruzzo offer rich histories without the crowds. These sites often provide a more intimate and personal experience, allowing you to delve deeper into Italy's past. Local guides at these lesser-known sites can offer fascinating stories and perspectives that enhance your understanding of the country's history.

Engage with Locals: Italians are known for their hospitality and love of conversation. Engaging with locals, whether through language exchange meetups, guided tours, or simply striking up a conversation in a café, can lead to unforgettable experiences and insider tips. Learning a few basic Italian phrases can help break the ice and show respect for the local culture. Participating in local activities, such as a community festival or a neighborhood market, can provide deeper connections and more meaningful interactions.

Stay in Family-Run Accommodations: Opting for family-run hotels, agriturismos, or bed-and-breakfasts can offer a more personalized and authentic experience. These accommodations often provide insights into local traditions, homemade meals, and warm hospitality. The owners can offer valuable recommendations for exploring the area and finding hidden gems that are off the typical tourist path.

Attend Local Workshops and Artisanal Shops: Italy is known for its craftsmanship in areas such as ceramics, glassblowing, and leatherwork. Attending workshops or visiting artisanal shops allows you to see these crafts in action and purchase unique, handmade items. Cities like Florence, Murano, and Sorrento are renowned for their artisans and provide opportunities to learn about traditional techniques and support local craftspeople.

10.2 Additional Resources

Planning a trip to Italy can be an exciting yet daunting task, given the wealth of attractions and experiences the country offers. Fortunately, there are numerous resources available to help travelers make the most of their Italian adventure. From apps and websites to books and movies, these resources provide valuable insights and practical information for exploring Italy.

Useful Apps and Websites

In the digital age, a range of apps and websites can enhance your travel experience in Italy:

Google Maps: Essential for navigation, finding restaurants, and exploring nearby attractions, Google Maps is a must-have app for any traveler. It provides real-time directions, reviews, and information on public transportation routes and schedules.

TripAdvisor and Yelp: Great for restaurant reviews, activity suggestions, and booking tours, these platforms allow users to read reviews from fellow travelers and make informed decisions about where to eat, stay, and visit. They also offer booking options for various tours and activities.

Rome2Rio: This app provides detailed information on how to get from one place to another using various modes of transportation, including trains, buses, ferries, and flights. It's particularly useful for planning trips between cities and regions.

Trenitalia and Italo: These are the official apps for Italy's primary train services, offering schedules, booking options, and real-time updates. Trenitalia covers the extensive national rail network, while Italo offers high-speed services between major cities.

Eatwith: Connects travelers with local hosts for unique dining experiences in their homes. This platform offers a range of culinary experiences, from home-cooked meals to cooking classes, providing an authentic taste of Italian cuisine.

Google Translate: Helpful for overcoming language barriers, especially in more remote areas. The app offers real-time translation of text, speech, and even images, making it easier to communicate with locals and navigate through menus, signs, and other written materials.

Culture Trip: This website and app provide curated travel guides and articles about destinations around the world, including Italy. It's a great resource for discovering lesser-known attractions, cultural tips, and insider recommendations.

MyTaxi (Free Now): An efficient way to book taxis in major Italian cities, ensuring reliable transportation and the ability to track your ride in real-time.

WhatsApp: Widely used in Italy for communication, this app is invaluable for staying in touch with local contacts, making reservations, and even coordinating with tour guides.

Books and Movies to Inspire Your Trip

Delving into Italian literature, history, and cinema can enrich your travel experience by providing context and inspiration:

Books:

Under the Tuscan Sun by Frances Mayes: A memoir about renovating a villa in Tuscany, offering insights into Italian life and culture.

A Farewell to Arms by Ernest Hemingway: A classic novel set during World War I, partially in Italy, exploring themes of love and war.

The Leopard by Giuseppe Tomasi di Lampedusa: A historical novel about a Sicilian noble family during the Risorgimento, capturing the complexities of Italian history.

Italian Neighbors by Tim Parks: A humorous and affectionate account of life in a small Italian village, shedding light on everyday Italian customs and traditions.

The Birth of Venus by Sarah Dunant: A historical fiction set in Florence during the Renaissance, filled with art, intrigue, and vivid descriptions of the city.

Movies:

La Dolce Vita (1960): Federico Fellini's masterpiece, capturing the essence of Rome in the 1960s with its glamorous yet decadent lifestyle.

The Talented Mr. Ripley (1999): A thriller set against the stunning backdrop of 1950s Italy, showcasing locations like Rome, Venice, and the Amalfi Coast.

Eat Pray Love (2010): Follows a woman's journey of self-discovery, starting in Italy, with beautiful scenes of Rome, Naples, and other iconic locations.

Cinema Paradiso (1988): A heartwarming film about a boy's love for cinema in a small Sicilian village, reflecting the cultural and social life of Italy.

Call Me by Your Name (2017): Set in the idyllic Italian countryside, this film explores a summer romance and the beauty of northern Italy.

Travel Guides and Online Resources

Lonely Planet Italy: This comprehensive travel guide offers detailed information on attractions, accommodations, and dining options across Italy. It's a valuable resource for planning your itinerary and learning about local customs and culture.

Rick Steves' Italy: Known for his approachable and practical travel advice, Rick Steves' guidebooks and TV shows provide insights into traveling like a local, with tips on hidden gems and must-see sights.

Fodor's Essential Italy: Another excellent travel guide that covers major cities and regions, providing recommendations on what to see, where to eat, and where to stay.

The Local Italy: An English-language news website that covers current events, cultural stories, and practical advice for living and traveling in Italy.

Italian Tourism Official Website: Offers official information on travel to Italy, including visa requirements, health and safety tips, and guides to major attractions and regions.

Cultural Immersion

Duolingo: A fun and interactive way to learn Italian, Duolingo offers free language lessons that can help you get comfortable with basic Italian phrases and vocabulary before your trip.

Cooking Classes and Wine Tasting: Look for online platforms offering virtual cooking classes and wine tasting sessions. These experiences can provide a deeper understanding of Italian culinary traditions and prepare you for the flavors you'll encounter during your travels.

Cultural Exchange Programs: Consider joining cultural exchange programs or homestay networks, such as Workaway or Couchsurfing, to experience Italian life from a local perspective.

10.2.1 Useful Apps and Websites
In the digital age, a range of apps and websites can enhance your travel experience in Italy:

Google Maps: Essential for navigation, finding restaurants, and exploring nearby attractions. Google Maps provides detailed directions, public transportation routes, and reviews of local businesses, making it an invaluable tool for any traveler.

TripAdvisor and Yelp: Great for restaurant reviews, activity suggestions, and booking tours. These platforms offer user-generated reviews and ratings, helping you make informed decisions about where to eat, what to see, and which tours to take.

Rome2Rio: Provides detailed information on how to get from one place to another using various modes of transportation. This app is particularly useful for planning complex journeys that involve multiple forms of transport, such as trains, buses, ferries, and flights.

Trenitalia and Italo: Official apps for booking train tickets and checking schedules. These apps allow you to purchase tickets, check train times, and receive updates on delays or cancellations, ensuring a smooth travel experience across Italy's extensive rail network.

Eatwith: Connects travelers with local hosts for unique dining experiences in their homes. This platform offers a range of dining options, from home-cooked meals to cooking classes and food tours, providing an authentic taste of local cuisine and culture.

Google Translate: Helpful for overcoming language barriers, especially in more remote areas. This app can translate text, speech, and even images of written words, making it easier to communicate and understand signs, menus, and other written materials.

WhatsApp: Widely used in Italy for communication. Having this app can help you stay in touch with local contacts, make reservations, and receive important updates from tour operators or accommodation providers.

Citymapper: Excellent for navigating public transportation in major cities like Rome, Milan, and Florence. This app provides real-time information on buses, trams, and trains, as well as walking and cycling routes.

10.2.2 Books and Movies to Inspire Your Trip
Delving into Italian literature, history, and cinema can enrich your travel experience by providing context and inspiration:

Books:

Under the Tuscan Sun by Frances Mayes: A memoir about renovating a villa in Tuscany, offering insights into Italian life and culture. Mayes' vivid descriptions of the Tuscan landscape, local traditions, and culinary delights provide a heartfelt and inspiring read.

A Farewell to Arms by Ernest Hemingway: A classic novel set during World War I, partially in Italy. Hemingway's narrative captures the beauty and tragedy of war, with evocative descriptions of the Italian countryside and cities.

The Leopard by Giuseppe Tomasi di Lampedusa: A historical novel about a Sicilian noble family during the Risorgimento. This richly detailed novel explores themes of change and continuity, providing a deep understanding of Sicily's history and culture.

Italian Neighbors by Tim Parks: A humorous and affectionate account of life in a small Italian village. Parks' observations on Italian customs, language, and daily life offer an entertaining and insightful look at living in Italy.

Movies:

La Dolce Vita (1960): Federico Fellini's masterpiece, capturing the essence of Rome in the 1960s. The film's portrayal of the glamorous yet empty lives of its characters offers a poignant reflection on fame, love, and the pursuit of happiness.

The Talented Mr. Ripley (1999): A thriller set against the stunning backdrop of 1950s Italy. The film's beautiful cinematography showcases Italy's scenic locations, from the bustling streets of Rome to the idyllic coastal towns.

Eat Pray Love (2010): Follows a woman's journey of self-discovery, starting in Italy. The film highlights the transformative power of travel and the beauty of Italian culture and cuisine.

Cinema Paradiso (1988): A heartwarming film about a boy's love for cinema in a small Sicilian village. This nostalgic and touching story celebrates the magic of movies and the bonds of friendship and community.

These resources can provide a deeper understanding and appreciation of Italy's culture, history, and lifestyle, making your trip even more meaningful and memorable. By following insider tips and utilizing helpful apps and websites, you can navigate Italy like a local and discover its hidden gems and authentic experiences. Exploring Italy with this enriched perspective will allow you to connect more deeply with the places you visit and create lasting memories.

Made in United States
Troutdale, OR
10/07/2024

23478140R00056